Five Steps to Freedom

*A Path to Inner Harmony and
Personal Growth*

PHIL GOLDING

BALBOA.
PRESS

A DIVISION OF HAY HOUSE

Balboa Press books may be ordered through booksellers or by contacting:

Balboa Press
A Division of Hay House
1663 Liberty Drive
Bloomington, IN 47403
www.balboapress.com.au
1-(877) 407-4847

ISBN: 978-1-4525-0305-9 (sc)
ISBN: 978-1-4525-0306-6 (e)

Because of the dynamic nature of the Internet, any web addresses or
links contained in this book may have changed since publication and
may no longer be valid. The views expressed in this work are solely those
of the author and do not necessarily reflect the views of the publisher,
and the publisher hereby disclaims any responsibility for them.

The author of this book does not dispense medical advice or prescribe
the use of any technique as a form of treatment for physical, emotional,
or medical problems without the advice of a physician, either directly
or indirectly. The intent of the author is only to offer information
of a general nature to help you in your quest for emotional and
spiritual well-being. In the event you use any of the information in
this book for yourself, which is your constitutional right, the author
and the publisher assume no responsibility for your actions.

Any people depicted in stock imagery provided by Thinkstock are
models, and such images are being used for illustrative purposes only.
Certain stock imagery © Thinkstock.

Printed in the United States of America

Balboa Press rev. date: 04/03/2012

This work is dedicated to spreading peace and self realization wherever possible.

ACKNOWLEDGMENTS

I thank everyone who has crossed my path in life. You are the rich source of experience that has enabled me to learn about life. Thanks also to all my clients and students who have given me the opportunity to transform my life experience into practical knowledge, and to place my experience into book form. Thanks to Paul Mischefski and Balboa Press for helping with editing.

I especially thank my darling wife, Osha, for sticking by me and supporting me in so many ways throughout this long project.

CONTENTS

Introduction xiii
 1. Perennial Wisdom xiii
 2. Personal Experience xiv
 The Right Approach to Healing xvi
THE 5-STEP PROCESS Synopsis xxi

The 5 STEP PROCESS

CHAPTER 1

Step 1. ACCEPTANCE 1
 Where Our Confusion Begins 1
 The Key That Frees Us From Suffering 7
 Exercise 1: Opening The Door To Love
  And Healing 9
 Love, The Ultimate Power 13
 Self-Acceptance Is Responsible Self-Care 20
 Reprogramming Our Childhood Conditioning 22
 Caring For Our Emotions 27
 Exercise 2: Be Your Own Loving Guardian 32
 Chapter One Summary 36

CHAPTER 2

*AWAKENING YOUR POTENTIAL FOR
HEALING AND POSITIVE CHANGE* 41
 Self-Awareness 41

Running On Ego   42
Conscious-Awareness   44
Human-Self   47
    Basic Character
        Base Instincts
        Emotions/Feelings
        Intellect—our ability to think
        Will
Inner-Child   50
Be The Wise Parent Of Your Human-Self   51
Chapter Two Summary   53

CHAPTER 3
Step 2. PERSONAL RESPONSIBILITY   57
Pride, Self-Righteousness, And Denial   59
The Victim Trap   61
The Question Of Justice   63
Justice Versus Revenge   66
Understanding Emotions   69
    1. Free Emotional Response
    2. Trapped Emotional Reaction
Take Ownership Of Your Life   75
5 Keys To Caring For Yourself   77

    1. Daily Journal
            Meditation
    2. Education and Inspiration
    3. Counselling / Therapy/ Life-Coaching
    4. Self-Awareness Groups
    5. Look After Your Body

Exercise 3: Separating Fact from Fiction   86
Chapter Three Summary   95

CHAPTER 4

Step 3. LET GO & TUNE IN   100

   A New Reality   100

   Letting Go   104

   Tuning In   109

      Learning to Feel

      Clarity

      Controlling the Breath

   The Quest For Healing   115

   Connecting To Your Higher Consciousness   122

   Exercise 4: Working with Emotions   123

   Chapter Four Summary   135

CHAPTER 5

Step 4. LIVING IN THE NOW   140

   Reality Is Now   140

   Worry, Regret, Guilt, And Resentment Ruins

      Your Future   143

      Accepting the Past and Gaining the Benefits

      The Destructive Power of Worry

   Human Beings Learn By Trial And Error   146

   Discipline, One Day At A Time.   148

      Goal Setting

      Creating Routines

   Joy And Serenity Is Now   154

   Exercise 5: Embracing the Day   158

   Chapter Five Summary   164

CHAPTER 6

Step 5. LIVE THE PROCESS AS A WAY OF LIFE   168

Appendix One   171

Appendix Two   175

About the Author   179

INTRODUCTION

What I have laid out for you in this book is a five step process for emotional healing, wisdom and empowerment. This book is an outline of a workable strategy for personal change. Those in the field of Transpersonal Psychology know such a strategy works for two main reasons.

1. PERENNIAL WISDOM

Firstly, we live in a wonderful age where we can gain access to recorded information that human beings have stored down through the ages. Humanity has produced many great philosophers and sages throughout history. What they have written can now be studied and compared in what is called a meta-analysis. What has been discovered is that their writings and teachings all correlate in fundamental ways. It is like there is a set of "natural laws" that apply not only to physics, but also to consciousness. This has been termed "perennial wisdom", which simply means wisdom that endures. When you apply these laws to your life, you naturally enter into a journey of emotional healing and mental clarity, as years of accumulated confusion unravels and falls away.

2. PERSONAL EXPERIENCE

Secondly, we know such processes work because enough of us have applied these laws of consciousness to our own lives and have experienced the benefits directly. There are still sections in the more orthodox psychology and medical profession that remain sceptical. There is a tendency to believe that evidence can only be gathered through statistical analysis in a laboratory, but the real world does not exist in a laboratory. Those in my field of Transpersonal Psychology regard life as the laboratory, although we still value orthodox scientific research. In addition though, we see ourselves as the experiment. We first apply these principles of personal change to ourselves, because if we can't put this to work in our own lives, how can we expect others to do the same, and how can we possibly know what it is really like? We endeavour to be less the out-of-touch expert and more the living example.

I personally had a difficult childhood for various reasons, which led to chronic depression in my teenage and early adult years. This depression further complicated my life by restricting my ability to make wise decisions on my own behalf, or I avoided making decisions altogether. I was stuck, and afraid to take a risk in life. This resulted in difficulties in my relationships and a career that did not reflect my true potential. At the age of 24 my chronic depression drove me to seek help, and I attended self-help groups regularly for the next twelve years, as well as some counselling. As I learned to put these principles for personal change to work, my life began to improve accordingly. I didn't reach out for as much help as I could have, but I kept steadily growing nonetheless.

Even though I soon learned to function well, whenever I took on a new challenge, my chronic depression would be triggered once again. Finally, after eight years of personal growth work that helped me in many other areas of my life, I decided to spend some dedicated time focusing on my depression and nothing else. Using all that I had learned, I surprised even myself by finally breaking the back of my depression in just few weeks. At the core of this shift in awareness was being awakened to the fundamental, unconditional worthiness of myself as a human being. I have a right to be on this planet, learning and growing as I make my way through life. This right applies to everyone. There is nothing we have to do to earn this right. I will speak more about this in the first chapter. The key that has enabled me to translate this awareness into a life-transforming strategy was a genuine commitment to ongoing self-acceptance and responsible self care.

I have experienced depressed feelings at times since then but I now know what to do about it. It can no longer take a hold of me. You could now say that I am immune to this chronic disorder. Of course I could have overcome my depression a lot sooner if I knew at 24 what I know now, but this was not the case. Besides, my experience has been my greatest teacher where becoming a psychotherapist is concerned. It has helped me learn that every problem can be turned into an opportunity.

An added benefit to my personal growth work was that as I continued to work on myself, my natural interest in psychology began to blossom. Before I knew psychotherapy was to be my career, I was already well versed in the subject.

My own higher consciousness knew this was my calling well before my mind was aware of it.

My own experiences of healing and personal development, along with helping others heal and grow, led to me developing what I simply call the "5 Step Process". This process reveals the natural laws of consciousness that facilitate mental and emotional wellbeing. The 5 Step Process is the foundation of all my counselling and personal development work and is the basis of this book.

Over the years of my professional career as a counsellor, psychotherapist, and meditation / personal development teacher, the 5 Step Process has more than proven its effectiveness. The truth of the core principles of the process have only been reinforced by the test of experience. I also put this process into practice in my personal life by continuing to develop myself, and in the way I approach my relationships with my wife and my two beautiful stepchildren.

THE RIGHT APPROACH TO HEALING

In-depth therapy and sharing are very important. Where serious emotional difficulties such as depression are concerned, there needs to be a commitment to long-term counselling. Such a commitment should be taken seriously if we expect to get results. Serious emotional imbalances rarely respond to "quick-fix" treatments. There may be some quick results, but the relief is often temporary because the treatment did not reach the required depth. If we have an expectation that the "cure" should be quick, we may assume the treatment is not working if this doesn't happen. Because of this our doubts and anxiety may interfere with our commitment to healing. We may jump from one therapist, self-help group or philosophy to the next without giving any of them the required time and commitment needed to work. Worse still, we may just lose hope and give up.

Instead of looking for the illusive cure, real positive results are more likely to be achieved if we approach emotional recovery as a change of lifestyle. This new lifestyle must be one of ongoing self-care, rather than self-neglect or self-rejection. Life will always have its difficulties, even in normal circumstances. It is unrealistic to think otherwise. Being self-responsible enough to learn the skills of ongoing mind-maintenance is essential for a well balanced and successful life.

Your commitment and persistence with a particular therapy or philosophy is as important as the therapy itself. After all, it is your mind and body. Your attitudes are with you always until you change them.

Where our emotional wellbeing is concerned, we human beings have an unhealthy tendency of not reaching out for help because we feel ashamed at not being able to cope. We think we have failed in some way if we can't do it alone. When we finally do reach out, we often expect the therapist to do all the work, to perform some sort of magic.

The "expert" can't be with you 24 hours a day. Counselling is most effective when counsellor and client come together as a team. This means working together to move you, the client, through your emotional blocks to a state of functioning that better matches your potential. The most important aspect of any therapy is to empower you with the skills and ability to take charge of your life in a positive, life-enhancing way. This book is an introduction to this fulfilling approach to life.

Just having someone to talk to, who is detached but caring, accepting, and objective is therapy in itself. However, emotional recovery also needs a pro-active approach if a genuine shift is going to take place. In other words, it is important to have an active strategy to tackle your negative thought-patterns and clear your stuck emotions. Such a strategy enables you to gain awareness of negative thought-patterns and then learn how to replace them with ones that work for you. Such a strategy is often called a "process". I use what is called a "5 Step Process", which underpins all my counselling and personal development work.

This may be a small book, but it has a lot of depth. These words and concepts are a product of my own personal experience. For it to truly make a difference to your life, it must be studied like a manual; not read like a novel and then put on the shelf. For a full understanding, it will require time and a willingness to put these principles into practice daily, and in so doing, slowly but surely master them. For this information to come alive in your heart and mind, you have to live it and experience it first hand.

The

5-STEP PROCESS

1. ACCEPTANCE

2. PERSONAL RESPONSIBILITY

3. LET GO AND TUNE IN

4. LIVE IN THE NOW

5. LIVE THE PROCESS AS A WAY OF LIFE

THE 5-STEP PROCESS SYNOPSIS

This process is used to directly work with your emotional wounds, fears, insecurities and confusion. It is designed to develop your self-awareness and your own compassionate relationship with yourself. This vital conscious connection to your own human self is the doorway to ongoing mental and emotional healing and development, which, in turn, leads to ever increasing self-empowerment and self-mastery.

Step 1. Acceptance

Without self acceptance, we cannot heal, find inner-peace, or grow. We often suffer because of our experience of being judged by other people. It is our own lack of acceptance of ourselves, however, that makes us vulnerable to the judgement from others. We often mistakenly think others are judging us when, in fact, we are judging ourselves. Every human being has fears and insecurities and gets confused. Every human being also has natural wisdom and a deep capacity to love. When we can accept both sides of ourselves, we can then consciously heal our emotional pain and confusion with our own higher-awareness. With self-acceptance, the doorway to our true potential opens to us. The power of self-acceptance is in knowing that our worthiness is without question. We all make mistakes. We are all learning and growing. In order to feel free, happy, and fulfilled, we must accept our fundamental worthiness as a human being. By unconditionally accepting ourselves as we are and caring for ourselves as best we can each day, we are then in a better position to accept and positively work with any challenges that we may face in life. Step 1 is connecting to our own internal source of love that is available to us always.

Step 2. Personal Responsibility

When we combine acceptance with Personal Responsibility, self-rejection is replaced with compassionate caring for our own humanness. Personal Responsibility means that we are in charge of our own lives; that we have the independent ability to stand on our own feet. In order to take charge of our lives, we must accept our Personal Responsibility to Love ourselves Unconditionally, knowing that achieving this goal is an ongoing process of learning. Facing our issues is much easier when choosing this approach. We stop wasting our time trying to control and change others in order to heal, grow and be happy. The key to our healing, inner-peace, happiness, and fulfilment is in our own hands. By living this new understanding as best we can each day, conflict and unhealthy dependency can be overcome, which naturally improves our relationships with those around us. The result is an increasing inner-harmony and self-empowerment. Step 2 is accepting full authority over our own lives and knowing that we have that capability.

Step 3. Let Go & Tune In

The key to happiness and empowerment is being able to confidently and skilfully take care of our own vulnerable human-selves. We achieve this by letting go of trying to control and punish other people or ourselves when emotional pain is triggered within us, knowing that self-rejection is the real cause of our pain. By accepting our personal responsibility to love ourselves unconditionally, we instead focus inwards on the disempowering confusion that has conditioned our minds. As we learn to correct these self-rejecting thought patterns and compassionately care for our own vulnerabilities, we discover our own power of wisdom and healing. As a result of our persistent efforts, we are increasingly released from pain and confusion and in the process, we gain an increasing experience of command over our own lives. As our hearts heal and open, we naturally attract and create more love and abundance. Step 3 is taking care of our own minds by putting Steps 1 and 2 into action.

Step 4. Live in the Now

When we get in touch with and accept responsibility for our needs and emotions, we are increasingly able to achieve the clarity of mind to take wise action on our own behalf. Another benefit of letting go and tuning in is that we recognise the futility of worry, regret and resentment. By working these steps, we discover how to learn from the past and achieve our goals by positively accepting and working with the reality that is in front of us and within us now. We realise that making peace with the past and creating a positive future is determined by the way we take responsible care of ourselves every day, one day at a time. We realise that we have full authority and power over our own minds and

PHIL GOLDING

therefore our lives. As a result of putting this understanding into action every day as best we can as we are learning and growing, our lives simplify, and our happiness and vitality increases. Self-empowerment and self-mastery becomes a real experience in our lives. Step 4 is by putting Steps 1, 2 and 3 into action on a daily basis. Step 4 is about knowing that the power to create the life that we want is contained within how we personally take care of each now moment.

Step 5. Live the Process

Step 5 is about committing to this new, empowered way of approaching life. The 5 Step Process becomes a healthy, sustainable and empowering lifestyle. By working these steps as an ongoing process, every problem becomes an opportunity to understand ourselves more, heal more deeply, gain more insight and grow stronger. As our skill in self-management increases, our faith and trust in ourselves increases. We grow in self-esteem and self-confidence. We attract and create healthier relationships and we better manage those relationships we have. Our ability for wise discernment continues to grow, enabling us to manage healthy personal boundaries in the face of life's challenges. By living this process as a way of life, we continue to evolve into our true potential. We soon have something to give back to the world, for we increasingly have love to spare. Life becomes truly meaningful and fulfilling. We are willing and able to embrace all that life contains. Step 5 is about knowing that we can benefit from every situation in life.

CHAPTER 1

STEP ONE
ACCEPTANCE

WHERE OUR CONFUSION BEGINS

The opposite of self-acceptance is negative self-judgment or self-rejection. This form of self-judgment, more than anything else, blocks us in our efforts to work through and overcome emotional problems.

In my personal and professional experience, all destructive judgement stems from one fundamental belief, or rather *misbelief*, that becomes imbedded in our minds from an early age. This misbelief is:

> ⊘ *I am unworthy because I am human.*

By the term "human", I mean not perfect. For children in particular, the standard of perfect behaviour is measured by others such as parents, teachers, older siblings, social pressure from peers or the media, or any other form of perceived authority. Furthermore, there are invariably many different versions of what this perfect standard is, depending on who is giving out the discipline, or the pressure to conform. This standard can even change from moment to moment with one individual disciplinarian, depending on his or her changing moods. When we were children, we were often unable to live up to these standards. Sometimes this was because we weren't given the appropriate training and mentoring, and sometimes it was because we simply lacked ability in that area. Sometimes the standards set for us were actually impossible to comply with.

We are very vulnerable when we are children. We are dependent on our adult carers for our physical, mental, and emotional wellbeing. In relation to our mental and emotional wellbeing, as children, we depend on our carers for our sense of identity and worthiness. It is essential for our successful development into adulthood that we feel we belong and that we are loved unconditionally. When we don't receive this vital love and attention, we are liable to be adversely affected in a very deep way.

During our childhood, when we failed to live up to the standards set for us by our carers, some of us suffered abuse, ridicule, and rejection. We were deemed unworthy of love. As a result, we frequently felt sad, afraid, ashamed, abandoned, angry, and so on.

Often the problem is a lack of active mentoring by our carers. They were often pre-occupied and/or absent and not in tune with our essential needs. We felt unworthy of love in this situation as well—not important to our carers. Feelings of loss, abandonment, and loneliness would be particularly strong as a result of this.

Another problem many of us faced in childhood was too much involvement from our carers. As children, we need room to be ourselves—to develop our own unique identities according to our own special potential. When our carers are overbearing and inappropriately controlling, we end up feeling inadequate, incapable and helpless. We tend to remain dependent on others, overly compliant to the demands of others, and unaware of what is uniquely and essentially important for our own needs. Our creativity and self-confidence becomes stifled. Our sense of what love is becomes highly distorted. There is always an underlying dread that we will be deemed unworthy of love and even abandoned if we dare to think and act for ourselves.

Another situation we can encounter as children is a home environment that is chaotic and even dangerous. We may not have known what to expect from one moment to the next. A sense of all-pervading fear and anxiety known as random conditioning is often the result. One minute we may be stroked and the next we may be beaten, without knowing why. At other times, we may be inappropriately left alone to fend for ourselves for extended periods of time. With this sort of unpredictability, our primal defences have to be on all the time. We need love like everyone else, but we become afraid of it as well. Love, in this situation, becomes a confusing nightmare.

As children, due to our vulnerable, undeveloped minds and resultant deep dependency, we end up taking such negative experiences very personally. Without even realising it, we conclude that we must be fundamentally wrong in some way to be treated in such a manner. In many ways we conclude that we don't deserve love. We take on the beliefs of our main carers, not knowing anything else. As children, we are on a rapid learning and developmental path, but we can't yet discern the quality of what we are learning. We are just unconsciously soaking it all up. This is the root of childhood conditioning, positive and negative. This deep misbelief that we are unworthy simply because we are human becomes embedded into our minds.

Love is repeatedly withdrawn from us when we are children, often simply for being childish. As children, we are placed in an impossible dilemma. Being children means that we have little capacity to control our instinctual cravings and emotions. We simply can't help ourselves. We are doomed to fail when we are expected to be "good little adults" by well-meaning but confused carers, or carers who are plainly abusive.

When we take this misbelief into adulthood, no matter how we try to hide this deep confusion from the world around us, it nevertheless pervades and distorts every area of our lives. This condemnation, this withdrawal of love, I believe, is the main root of all continuing rejection of ourselves and others.

As children, we may have also had a character that was sensitive or difficult to manage, in many different ways, which can compound the situation. In other words, children often display strong personality traits and emotional dispositions seemingly from birth. We are not necessarily a blank slate before we start. Nevertheless, the weight of responsibility is on parents and other significant carers to equip themselves with the skills for the task of parenthood. It is the parents' challenge to constructively work with their child's negative traits to help the child reduce them or even overcome them. It is also an opportunity for the parents to help the child reach his or her highest potential. Children are children. They cannot be expected to successfully parent themselves.

As powerless, vulnerable children, we are so dependent on our carers that we are compelled to try to conform to their confusion no matter how impossible this may be to achieve. In the face of this dilemma, we feel so powerless and unworthy that we are inclined to believe negative judgments about ourselves, even though in our hearts it doesn't feel right.

Naturally, all children need guidance and discipline. This is how we learn to take control of our own emotions and needs. All discipline, however robust it may need to be at times, must be wise, loving and compassionate. Otherwise it contains elements of destructiveness.

Of course, the withdrawal of love is where the confusion starts for everyone, and we all then pass it down the line from generation to generation. Because we are all human, no-one is a perfect parent. Coming to terms with our humanness as parents is one of the real challenges of personal development. In reality, children don't need perfect parents. What children need are parents who are self-aware and who can take care of their own humanness, instead of projecting their fears and insecurities onto their children. Of course, as parents, we are going to frequently make mistakes. It is essential, therefore, to openly accept our mistakes, face them and learn from them. This then becomes the best example for our children. They learn to accept and care for their own humanness.

When we were children, we may not have had an appropriate example of self-care to relate to, so we grew to regard self-rejection as a normal way to think. Because of this "normalizing", these self-destructive judgments become embedded deep within our minds where they continue to control us beyond our awareness. Because of this "normalizing", negative subconscious thought-patterns gain a hold in the early stages of childhood development and grow into distorted beliefs that then control how we think, feel, and act. These misbeliefs then keep our emotional problems on a repetitive loop, creating ongoing difficulties such as conflict, when conflict wouldn't be present otherwise. Our perceptions of reality become distorted. We then continue to create a distorted reality for ourselves throughout our lives until we become aware of these self-defeating beliefs and change them. Until then, we may think that life is against us, but in actual fact it is our own negatively programmed minds that are causing our suffering.

As a result of this confusion, we think being mistreated by others is the cause of our suffering, as it was when we were children. However, as adults, it is our own self-rejection, emerging out of our own misbeliefs, that makes us so emotionally vulnerable to the perceived or actual mistreatment from others.

This fundamental insight can be very difficult to comprehend at first. We have been so conditioned to blame others for our emotional suffering. On the surface it appears so convincing that someone else or something else is the cause. We think that if only they would behave in the way we think they should, everything would be all right. Sometimes the other person's behaviour is destructive. More often than not though, we have misread the situation. More often than not we are over-reacting to someone's minor human imperfections. More often than not, people don't intend to hurt us, they are just a bit unskilful at times, just like you and I. Most often, the problem is not the other person. The problem lies in our inappropriate reactions to their humanness, and underneath that, to our own humanness.

As a result of our confusion, when it is time to deal with an issue that *does* need to be acted upon, we are not able to do this effectively. We either overreact or do not act at all. Caring for ourselves and being empowered is about learning to act appropriately. It is about consciously and confidently responding to life's challenges, rather than blindly and fearfully reacting in ways that just makes things worse.

Thinking that we are a victim and lashing out at others or ourselves or avoiding life's challenges altogether is self-defeating. This is the sort of thinking that is indicative of the confusion that keeps us believing we are powerless to control our own happiness and wellbeing.

THE KEY THAT FREES US FROM SUFFERING

In our confusion we are still relating to life from the position of being powerless children. In reality, an adult with a healthy self-esteem can shield his or herself from emotional suffering, or at least quickly recover, regardless of the negativity of the situation. Those with a healthy self-esteem carry a strong belief in their own self-worth. They are not dependent on others to give them permission to feel worthy. They do not need pats on the back before they can feel good about themselves. They already know they are worthy, even when they make human mistakes, which human beings inevitably do. Because of this strong belief in their essential worthiness, people who have a healthy self-esteem do not indulge in self-rejection and as a result, are less likely to be condemning of others. Those with a healthy self-esteem are psychologically protected by their own self-acceptance.

If we didn't first reject ourselves, acute emotional vulnerability in adulthood would not be there in the first place. Without this prior self-rejection, the condemnation from another would have little impact. We would simply know that the person doing the condemning is perhaps having a bad day and is obviously confused. We would know that no matter what mistakes we may happen to make, we do not deserve to be mistreated. We would know that we do not deserve to be condemned as unworthy.

We can't always have control over the behaviour of another. We can, however, take charge of what we accept into our own minds and hearts. We can shield ourselves with our own self-acceptance. Self-acceptance contains the power of love, which is far more powerful than most people realise.

An adult has the power of reasoning and the capacity of consciousness to know what feels right, and to trust that feeling. The only thing that feels right is love, along with all its qualities. As a result of our level of accumulated confusion, unfortunately for many of us, our ability to access this important adult capacity of conscious-awareness becomes impaired. We become so confused that we think we have to reject ourselves instead of love ourselves. This self-rejection locks us into a position of acute vulnerability. We become isolated from our own higher knowing. In our state of vulnerability, our limited survival instincts may then be inclined to condemn and attack as a form of "defence" in a blind reaction to the negative conditioning in our own minds.

Self-acceptance lifts us out of this unnecessary fight-or-flight reaction. Self-acceptance, lived in a consistent, dedicated way, inevitably dismantles and overcomes self-rejection and all its negative consequences.

A profound degree of self-acceptance is the key that frees us from suffering, whether your suffering comes in the form of depression, stress, anxiety, grief, anger, trauma—in fact any form of mental/emotional suffering—but there are many obstacles along the way to finally turning that key, and almost all of them are inside our own minds. This is why it can be so hard at first to see the true nature of these obstacles, and why it can be even harder to change them.

Don't be discouraged though. The fact that the obstacles are inside your own mind makes the situation easier, providing your healing journey is approached in the right way. It is made easier, because you don't have to waste your time trying to control or change other people. To find peace, happiness, and fulfilment, you only have to look within yourself. Almost all the changes you need to make are within your grasp. Furthermore, the unlimited power with which you need to make those changes is within you also.

The more we truly accept ourselves, the more we love ourselves unconditionally. The more we love ourselves unconditionally, the more we heal ourselves. The more we heal ourselves, the more self-aware and empowered we become and the more we are able to act in a way that is for our highest good.

EXERCISE 1:
OPENING THE DOOR TO LOVE
AND HEALING

Here is a contemplation exercise that may help you better comprehend the nature of self-acceptance, leading to unconditional love, and how to put it into practice in your life. (Fill in the blanks with the right gender for you to make it more personal.)

Imagine yourself as a newborn baby laying on a bed with you as your adult self looking down at this delicate, vulnerable, and precious being. Now as you are looking down at this beautiful little being, can you say in your heart that there is anything about this baby that is unworthy of Love? Can this baby do anything that makes it truly unworthy of Love? For instance, ... may frequently wake you up during the night by crying. . . . . may also dirty . . . . nappy a number of times per day. Neither of these experiences is very pleasant to have to deal with as the carer of this baby. Is the baby still worthy of Unconditional Love even when . . . . acts this way? Some people actually get angry at this unconscious behaviour of a new born baby. Is the problem with the baby or the carer?

Now your child is one-year-old and crawling around, getting into whatever . . . . can reach. Sometimes this little toddler is difficult at meal times, and can still keep you up at night. Your toddler is just doing what a toddler does. Is there anything about . . . . that is unworthy of Unconditional Love?

Now your toddler is a delightful two-year-old and becoming a real handful. . . . . . is now walking and therefore getting into more things. There is a lot of boundary testing going on as your toddler exercises . . . . awakening self-will in fits of defiance. This little one is also starting to talk in the cute way that toddlers do. Is there anything about this child that is undeserving of Unconditional Love? Would anyone be justified in getting angry at and judging this toddler if . . . . accidentally knocked over and broke that prized porcelain jug that you got for your wedding? Again, this child is just doing what a two-year-old does. If the carer gets angry at the child, where does the problem lie—with the carer or the child?

Now your child is five, very active and talking fluently. Even though . . . . is still quite the bundle of love, there is already some negative conditioning evident in this child's mind. You are already having a tussle with your child's newly forming ego. And yet even now this five-year-old is just doing what a five-year-old does. Where does the responsibility for the child's social conditioning lie—with the child or the child's carers? Has the child conditioned . . . . self? Again, is there anything unworthy about this five-year-old child? Is the child still worthy of Unconditional Love, a child who is still so vulnerable and dependent on the quality of care that . . . . receives?

And now you are watching yourself as a ten-year-old, playing with friends and going to school. Your child freely interacts with the rest of the family, a unique personality clearly emerging. . . . . is full of hopes and dreams for the future and yet still vulnerable and dependent. There is often conflict with brothers and sisters as your ten-year-old competes for love and approval. Negative conditioning is clearly visible. Deep behaviour patterns have been well established. Still this ten-year-old is just doing what a ten-year-old does. Is this growing child still worthy of Unconditional Love? If a carer withdraws their love from this child, where does the problem lie?

Now you are watching yourself as a fifteen-year-old, well into puberty and the new social scene. Your adolescent self is spending less time with family and instead seeking peer approval in . . . . own social group, sometimes in defiance of parental guidance. This leads to frequent conflict. . . . . is now experiencing the first forays into dating and relationships with its inevitable excitement and at times crushing disappointment. Your adolescent self is often moody and even behaves a bit oddly as . . . . searches for an independent identity. Childhood conditioning is now deeply entrenched and overlaid onto this youth's natural character. Again, your adolescent self is just doing the best that . . . . can. Should your adolescent self be judged for that? Should guidance come with condemnation or Unconditional Love?

How would it have been if you were given Unconditional Love all through your childhood? How would it have been if you felt safe to share your deepest fears, emotions, joys, and dreams with your parents all through your childhood and received nothing but loving guidance, caring, wise discipline, and encouragement that never made you wrong as a person? Isn't this what we deserve as children, no matter how many mistakes we made or how confused we may have become at times? How can a child be held responsible for . . . . own upbringing? Surely the responsibility lies with the carer.

Even as an adult this same rule applies. Even having to firmly say no to a person's confused and misguided behaviour can be done without withdrawing Unconditional Love.

When you look inside yourself now, you are looking at and feeling this child, a child that is still looking for, longing for that unconditional loving acceptance. You can find this child in your most vulnerable emotions. You are now the adult and this "inner-child" now belongs to you. Your carers did the best they could. Their job is now over. Now it is up to you. How have you been treating your child-self? How would it be if you lovingly accepted yourself unconditionally in a real heartfelt responsible way, instead of judging yourself and mistreating yourself whenever you make a human mistake, or don't supposedly measure up?

Even as an adult we are just doing the best we can. Mistakes are a natural part of being human. This deep form of self-acceptance enables us to wake up from our blind judging and blaming and instead consciously embrace and care for our vulnerable human-selves. With self-care, healing and growth are inevitable, along with maturity and wisdom. It is through self-acceptance that we can increasingly awaken our consciousness into higher states where it unites with Unconditional Love and therefore the power to heal the deepest fears and confusions.

After recognizing that there is a problem with the way we are approaching our life, acceptance is the first step in taking action to do something about it. This first step of acceptance is applied on many levels. Accepting the natural reality of our humanness is an essential part of step 1. It is the foundation for healing, and enables us to look at ourselves and life in an effective, constructive, and empowering way.

LOVE, THE ULTIMATE POWER

It is quite normal to assume that our only hope of escape from this nexus of suffering that self-rejection causes is to find someone who is willing to love us unconditionally, even when we are unable or unwilling to love them the same way in return. Surely we should be able to find refuge from suffering in a relationship with some ideal person.

This is another unrealistic expectation that leads to inevitable conflict and disillusionment. We expect others to make us happy. We even demand that they do so. We want someone who is safe, predictable and who satisfies our essential needs. Instead we end up with a human being with flaws, with fears, with insecurities, just like ourselves. This won't do of course, so we become locked in a struggle to control and change other people in order to feel loved, not realizing that we are choking love instead. So many relationships that are full of promise are destroyed because of our human confusion about the true nature of love.

As a consequence of all our confusion, love is regarded as a mystery, but it isn't really. From the perspective of Perennial Wisdom, love can be regarded as a science, and the most studied and mastered science of all. If love is regarded as a universal force, like light or gravity, then we can begin to look at it very differently. You don't need permission from somebody to receive light, freely given from the sun. Gravity is a natural part of everybody's experience. Why can't love be the same? If love is a science, it must have its own physics—a set of natural laws that can be understood and utilised for the benefit of our own wellbeing.

The problem lies in the fact that we have mistakenly come to believe that we can only receive love if someone else gives it to us. This is a natural psychological position for a child. Being a child means we are acutely vulnerable and deeply dependent on our fallible carers. When we didn't live up to the expectations of our carers, we often experienced having their love withdrawn from us. As a result, we felt rejected and abandoned. We are in such a vulnerable state as a child. Our natural attachment needs are so great that we often think we are being rejected and abandoned even when our carers are doing their best to love us. For example, one of our parents may pass away, or suffer a prolonged illness. Even through unavoidable circumstances, we can miss out on the care we need.

If these feelings of abandonment occur too often and remain unresolved, the result is a growing belief that we are unworthy of love. This misbelief then blocks our ability to love ourselves. When this misbelief continues to influence our minds, we develop an even deeper dependency on the love from others. We feel empty and needy of love. We come to believe that others have the power over our love. We remain feeling like a vulnerable child, even in adulthood. We are needy for love, but we are at the same time afraid of it. This fear of not receiving love then triggers our ego defences. We don't love ourselves, and we are afraid of other people because they may not give us the love that we so desperately need. Just as we can put up an umbrella to block out the rays of the sun, we have unconsciously constructed a mental umbrella that blocks out the vital *life-force* of love.

Our confusion about love is such a factor in our human experience that our misbeliefs have become ingrained in our collective human psyche. Even with a stable, happy childhood, we are still deeply influenced by this confusion about love. We don't realise that this love that we are trying to get from others is a second hand love, and often a worn-out, neglected love at that—worn-out and neglected because of their self-neglect.

What if our love wasn't actually owned by somebody else? That question requires some deep thought to grasp its significance.

To solve this riddle, we must re-examine the way we look at love. The common mistake we make is in thinking that we should be able to guarantee a sustainable love from another person, place or thing. Let's drop the places and things for the moment. We will look at that shortly. What about getting love from someone else? To lift the veil off this confusion we must deeply examine the above question. How can someone else own our love? Who gave them our love?

If this is the case, we must own the love that belongs to someone else. Where did we get that from? What do we really know about someone else's requirements for love and fulfilment? Do we even know what our own requirements are? If we are really honest with ourselves, we end up concluding that our awareness of this is vague at best. And yet human beings do love, and with great power.

Where I am getting to here is that we don't really know about love with any real awareness until we can truly love ourselves. I am talking here about loving ourselves unconditionally, which means being able to face and accept and work with everything about ourselves, even the parts of ourselves that we would rather hide away from the rest of society.

Occasionally we are fortunate enough to experience being in the presence of someone who does love unconditionally. It feels so wonderful. We feel so accepted and free when we are in their presence. But then they are gone again, and we are once again left feeling empty, even more so after having such an experience. We feel empty because we are looking for this love somewhere outside ourselves.

We so desperately look outside ourselves for love because of the depth of our own self-rejection.

The pressure to perform—to measure up has become so great in our society that our socially-conditioned minds are stuffed full of self-condemnation about all the little and big ways we do not measure up. This also means we blame others for not measuring up, which is really the same thing. We have an inner-tyrant constantly whipping us for our so-called failings. You don't think so? Try this personal experiment and see what you find.

Today, right this moment, make a rock solid commitment to treat yourself and speak to yourself only with loving kindness, compassion, forgiveness, and acceptance. Keep this up for the next seven days. Keep a little notebook in your pocket or your handbag and jot down every time you put yourself down. When you catch yourself, imagine this human-self that you are putting down is a vulnerable child just trying to grow. Do your best to find a way to mentor yourself and care for yourself in that moment in a kind and constructive way.

Be prepared to be shocked by how many times you put yourself down in a day. Be prepared to discover how unskilled you are at being your own wise, loving parent. Accept that also and just keep learning about yourself and the true nature of love through this process. Keep trying your best to love yourself unconditionally. After all, this is what unconditional love does. Concentrate on accepting your humanness as a part of loving yourself and let everyone else just be themselves.

When doing this experiment, you may get quick positive results. You may, however, run into confusion and pain. Don't be discouraged by this, as hard it may seem. What I suggest is happening is that you are running hard up against your self-condemnation programs. They are too strong at the moment to allow you to love yourself and actually feel the benefits of this exercise. The benefits will come if you don't give up, but you may need to reach out for help from a good counsellor or mentor.

What this exercise is about is being the wise, loving parent to your own fragile, vulnerable, confused, and often frightened human-self.

Doing this experiment for a week is just a taste. This probably won't be enough to turn your life around. Old, bad habits are harder than that to break. It will, nevertheless, be enough to reveal the reasons for much of your emotional pain. To turn your life around, you need to make living the principles of self-acceptance your new lifestyle. When you genuinely do this, you will place yourself in the position to just keep on learning and growing. When you do this, success is then inevitable. See Exercise 2, "Be Your Own Loving Guardian", at the end of this chapter for a more detailed description of this exercise.

Given the right love and skilful mentoring as a child, we actually grow up naturally having the ability to genuinely love ourselves in a healthy, responsible way, independent of anyone else. This is the healthy self-esteem that is created by loving and positive childhood conditioning. We have learned to love ourselves unconditionally to a high degree and therefore we are *in love* all the time! This capacity for a healthy self-esteem points to the fact that love can be accessed internally and not only from somewhere outside ourselves.

With the right approach and with persistence, we are able to access love directly from a universal source within our own self. Once we grow to a certain level of mental maturity, or conscious-awareness, to put it another way, we gain the ability to access this universal, internal love, regardless of the wounding and negative conditioning we experienced in childhood, or at any other time. As the adults we are now, we can identify the confusion about love that has accumulated in our minds throughout our formative years. Armed with this self-awareness, we can literally heal our memories and reprogram our minds to be in tune with the natural laws of love, thus establishing within our minds a healthy self-esteem, even when we didn't receive that in childhood.

I have personally experienced doing just that, and so have countless others throughout the history of humanity, and particularly now in this day and age. I have experienced, along with this rising tide of an awakening humanity, love as a life-force that I can freely access at any time, regardless of how humanly imperfect I may be at any given moment and regardless of my circumstances and conditions.

No one owns my love. All that I need to do to qualify for this Unconditional Universal Love is to exist! That's it! This is the reality for you as well, and for every human being. For many of us, this is a radical way of looking at love.

We are born from this love, we are born into this love, we live within this love, and we die back into this love.

I am not trying to preach to you here. What I am doing is offering you a scientific perspective on the reality of love as a universal life-force. I am offering you a very powerful hypothesis. Sincerely try the experiment and experience it for yourself.

We can love and heal ourselves because there is something about our human consciousness that enables us to get above our vulnerable, wounded human mind. Instead of being controlled by our conditioned minds; we can consciously and constructively take charge of our lives.

In reality, relationships succeed, and personal fulfilment is achieved, not only because other people love us, but because we possess a healthy form of self-love. This healthy self-love provides us with an inner-peace and openness that makes forming loving and healthy relationships with others a natural outcome. Fear and condemnation forces, controls, and attacks. Love and acceptance encourages, inspires and supports. Which of these spaces would you prefer to live in? Which would you prefer to create, for yourself and for others? The laws of love are very clear when it comes to how we treat ourselves.

We can examine and take a lesson from the lives of certain famous people who supposedly had it all, but suffered depression, loneliness and self-neglect, such as Marilyn

Monroe, Elvis Presley, Tammy Wynette and Michael Jackson, just to name a few. They were so loved and admired by so many people. What they also had in common was that they did not love themselves. They did not accept their own humanness.

Whenever we choose to accept ourselves as we are, we experience love. We are literally "in love". The love is always there. We are just opening up our hearts and minds to it and letting it in. In this atmosphere of self-acceptance, we can more effectively love others unconditionally, because we are no longer so afraid of not getting love. We are less afraid of not getting love because we already have it direct from the universal source of love. In such moments, we can also better receive the love that is offered to us by others. We can give them the freedom to be human, to be themselves, which makes giving and receiving love much easier.

This is about learning to be comfortable, happy, and free in your own skin. By cultivating this healthy form of self-love, every other aspect of your life is also enhanced.

SELF-ACCEPTANCE IS RESPONSIBLE SELF-CARE

Often I hear people remark, "Isn't all this talk about self-love really just about being selfish. Surely we should concentrate on loving others."

I am not talking about selfishness, I am talking about self-responsibility. I am talking about taking adult responsibility for our own emotional wellbeing. I am talking about the importance of establishing a healthy self-esteem that flows from a sustainable internal source. This does not take from anyone or anything.

The goal of a healthy self-esteem has become misunderstood and regarded as an excuse for self-indulgence. It has become associated with, and appropriated by, the belief that the more we believe in ourselves, the more material things we should give ourselves. The trouble here is that material things cannot sustain emotional fulfilment, but we have been led to believe that it can. This misbelief has been driven by consumerism and has led to social degradation on many levels. To be "normal" now means being a successful consumer. The social consequences have been, for a start, an increase in crime. "If I can't get it, I'll have to take it." Another consequence is depression on an epidemic scale. "I can't have it, or I have lost it, therefore I have failed." A third consequence is self-indulgence. "I have plenty of money, so that makes me worthy, so I can have all that I want, and I have to keep having it because enough is never enough."

To gain enough in order to keep getting enough, we have invented the rat-race where education and work is concerned. Fulfilment has become externalized to something outside us that we have to get, and you can throw relationships, sex, power, status and so on in there as well. We have turned life into a commodity, and in the process we have become consumer junkies.

The result of this approach to self-improvement is a society of people who are continually running on empty, where real love is concerned. When this is the case, we try to fill ourselves up by taking from others, or from the environment in destructive ways. This taking, this unhealthy dependency and endless materialism, loses touch with the important things in life. For instance, we think our children need more and more sophisticated toys rather than the essential life-blood of unconditional love. As a result, we confuse our children so much that they become dependent on more and more material things without realizing that it is unconditional love that they are really longing for. In the process, they don't learn how to love themselves and instead stay dependent on other people, places and things. When self-esteem is dependent on something external, it is always on very shaky ground. We become disconnected with the very core of our own greater self and self-neglect is the inevitable result. In reality, a lack of responsible self-love leads to selfishness and self-indulgence.

I believe, and it has been my long and repeated experience, that if we consciously and consistently accept and take care of our vulnerable human-selves, like one should lovingly and responsibly care for a child, we then naturally open up to, and experience, higher states of consciousness. These higher states of consciousness include inner peace, compassion, loving kindness, and creative motivation geared to the wellbeing of the wider community. If we don't care for ourselves in this healthy, sustainable way, we risk living our lives being blindly driven to destruction by the endless neediness of a confused and empty inner-child. At the very least, we won't reach our potential.

REPROGRAMMING OUR CHILDHOOD CONDITIONING

There are many factors that influence our lives and many of these factors are beyond our control, such as the environment we were born into, the forces of nature, or even our natural born character. The inevitable conditioning of our childhood can appear to be like another of these uncontrollable factors of our life, and indeed old habits can be hard to change.

Our childhood conditioning is a major determining factor in our lives, and for most people it is perhaps *the* major determining factor. It is with us twenty-four hours a day and can influence every aspect of our thinking, feeling, and action. It greatly determines the quality of our beliefs, which determines the quality of our relationships and choices in general. The negative side to this conditioning is the dominant cause of our fears and insecurities. Because this conditioning is so ingrained in us, we often assume we were born this way, as though it is a fixed part of our character, but this is not so.

In an attempt to overcome the negative influences of this deep childhood conditioning, we are likely to try many things, such as moving to a new location, getting a new job, ending a relationship, going on a diet, and so on. Sometimes this is enough. Often it isn't. Often our conditioning continues to interfere with our lives, creating the same old results, no matter what changes we make. If this is the case, our self-defeating conditioning must be reprogrammed into belief systems that are self-loving and life-enhancing. These new positive belief systems must become the new habits that our minds rely on.

If the old self-defeating programs are allowed to continue on unabated, some form of emotional breakdown can be the result, perhaps leading to antisocial and irrational behaviour, poor decision making, substance abuse, and so on. It is essential to heed the warning signs and reach out for help.

As hard as it may at first seem, changing our conditioning is most definitely achievable, but it must me approached in the right way. This self-change must come in the form of ongoing self-care. It is a conscious loving and caring relationship with our own humanness. We are creating a new, accepting, caring environment of self-awareness and self-love for our inner-child (vulnerable human-self) to grow up in.

Be aware that we are not changing ourselves to please others or to just conform. We are learning to make positive and empowered decisions on our own behalf—decisions that lead to self-respect and therefore respect from others.

One way of looking at this human self of ours is to recognize it as a most amazing, sensitive, powerful, one-of-a-kind creature, a bit like the horse we depended on in the past. Unlike the horse though, or the car we drive today, we can't trade this one in. This human-self, along with its mind, is our vehicle, and our home, for our whole life. It does not make sense to regard our human-selves as not worth looking after. When this priceless self in not running as it should, it is then a matter of objectively and carefully examining it in order to correct the problem. Also, it would be only logical to want to give this most precious self ongoing care and attention. For various reasons, however, we human beings tend to resist taking care of ourselves, as though we shouldn't need it, as though someone else should be magically doing it for us. We think such maintenance is an imposition on our lifestyle, particularly when it comes to caring for our own minds. It is little wonder we end up breaking down.

To extend the horse analogy a little further, our conscious-awareness is like the rider, the owner of the horse. We didn't train the horse. It was given to us already trained, just like we didn't bring ourselves up so much as being brought up by others. By the time we are adults, our conditioning is ours to reckon with. In the same way, it is like we are given this horse that somebody else trained, without being given adequate training in horse riding. We just have to get to know the horse and learn how to ride it. Like the owner and rider of the horse, we need to get to know our own minds and learn how to care for and manage our minds. It is no good complaining about this fact. It just is the way it is. The good thing is that we have the ability to do this, and facing the challenge and committing to it gives us the opportunity to develop invaluable life-long skills. There is nothing to lose by accepting this commitment and everything to gain, such as the control over our own lives and future.

Comparing our minds to a computer is a good analogy as well. As a computer, our human potential seems to be unlimited. The limitations are in the programming. Even though we have been programmed by someone else, as an adult, our capacity for conscious-awareness gives us the ability to be the computer and the computer programmer, both at the same time.

Often we *do* try to take care of ourselves but we have not learned how to do this effectively. When it comes to looking after our own minds, our emotions are often what are most difficult to handle. For too many of us, appreciating and looking after our human emotions is a mystery. The usual way we seem to treat our emotions is to run away from them or shut them down or shove them onto somebody else. We must learn how to skilfully manage and care for our emotional life. When properly understood and handled, emotions are a wonderful opportunity for great wisdom and inner-strength.

As a result of years of self-neglect, there is often a backlog of emotional energy waiting to be cleared. It is advisable to consciously and carefully let out the build-up of this emotional dam before the dam bursts with inevitable negative consequences. These negative out-of-control emotions may include fear, depression, anger, guilt, grief, shame, anxiety and stress etc. If allowed to continue unchecked, an emotional build-up can lead to substance abuse and other forms of addictions, relationship conflict or breakdown, child abuse, feelings of suicide, and other such serious consequences. In my experience, help is initially needed in order to safely release this emotional pressure. Further help is then needed to learn how to take effective care of our emotional self on an ongoing basis.

Because of our great potential, which comes with great complexity and sensitivity, we easily get out of tune. This is simply a fact of life. Self-rejection can severely hamper our ability to look at this fact of life objectively. Self-rejection says that we have failed in some way if we have to stop and do some maintenance on ourselves. This is an attitude that needs to be carefully examined. As a result of this self-defeating attitude, we may not make the needed effort to find the type of care that is appropriate for us and then stick with it. We must accept our humanness, along with our genuine need to reach out for help when it is required.

To accept someone as they are is to regard them as worthy of love no matter what. This is essential for the success of any intimate relationship or real friendship.

You must become your own best friend, your own loving guardian. This means that as a human being you regard yourself as worthy of unconditional love always, no matter who you are, what mistakes you have made, or what anyone has ever said about you or done to you. You must be your own essential source of unconditional love. This is the foundation of emotional health. This conscious approach to yourself and your life, along with a never-give-up, always open to learn attitude ensures that the positive reprogramming of your mind is inevitable.

CARING FOR OUR EMOTIONS

Rarely in our life do we experience being loved unconditionally. This is the reality of human confusion and limitation. We cannot control the misbeliefs of other people, but we can make a choice to love ourselves unconditionally. But here again we run up against our own human confusion and limitation. We have become habitually and blindly convinced that we should reject ourselves. We need to recognize that this self-rejection is an insidious form of violence that poisons our whole society.

Many of us deny our self-rejection by blaming others for our emotional pain. Nevertheless, the root of blame is non-acceptance of our humanness and our essential worth as a human being. When we deny our own humanity, we are then naturally prone to deny the humanity in others.

This self-rejection becomes a barrier to facing our negative conditioning and the emotional pain it causes. The problem, therefore, essentially lies with the way we sum up every situation. It is about what we believe each event means in relation to our own worthiness. When we suffer, we are unwittingly summing up these situations in ways that cause our own pain. Our ongoing confusion then causes us to hang onto this pain, because we don't understand that it is self-inflicted. As a result of this unconscious self-abuse, we do our best to avoid looking into ourselves. When we do, we are beaten up by our own self-rejection. In order to function, we keep ourselves continually distracted in an attempt to avoid feeling this self-inflicted pain. This is another very important concept that requires a lot of thought.

As a result of our lack of awareness of what we are doing to ourselves, we look for the cause of our pain in the things that are happening around us. We think it is the way others treat us, or the things we miss out on, or the thousand other things in our lives that "appear" to be causing our pain. All the while, the pain is really caused by what we think of ourselves in relation to our daily circumstances and conditions. This is why blaming the world never seems to resolve anything. This is why, as human beings, we feel so vulnerable at times.

Of course we need to deal with the various matters that confront us in our daily lives in order to protect our livelihood and wellbeing. Being able to manage our own affairs effectively and peacefully, however, totally depends on how deeply we understand that our worth as human beings is without question, no matter what the circumstances or conditions. When we understand this fundamental reality, our deep primal fear of being cast out and deprived of love subsides. We are in love all the time, because we live and function within the embrace of our own loving regard for ourselves. We have woken up a greater dimension of ourselves that has the power to be the representative of Universal Love to our own vulnerable human-selves.

When we are practicing self-acceptance, we are able to recognize that any thought that is not about loving ourselves unconditionally is confusion and should not be believed. Self-rejection is like the confusion of a child still learning about life. As a parent, we are not going to take for granted everything our five-year-old child says to us. Children naturally get confused, and so do our adult minds, because most of our embedded programming occurred when we were children. We are all still learning about life. This learning does not stop just because we walk around in adult bodies.

Observe, without judging, how a small child thinks, and you will gain more of an understanding of what is going on in your own subconscious mind when it emotionally reacts.

With self-acceptance, we learn to step back enough to see our emotional vulnerability for what it is—a scared, confused child needing help. Instead of rejecting and condemning this child, our confused, vulnerable, and hurting human-selves, we can instead have compassion for our own emotional pain. It is then easier to sit with it, to be with it, like we are gently holding this vulnerable child within us. We learn to not believe in the confused thoughts that want to attack ourselves or others, just like a hurt child lashing out. We instead recognise the fear and pain behind the anger and confusion. With this awareness, we can explore our vulnerability with activities such as writing our thoughts and feelings out in our journal, talking it over with a friend/mentor/counsellor, and reading some self-help material. As we are caring for our inner-child, our humanness, with self-acceptance, compassion, and self-responsibility, the blocked up emotional pain can be more effectively freed and safely released. It is easier to let the pain naturally flow and then let it go. Self-rejection and another one of its counterparts, self-pity, are transformed into self-care. Emotional healing is then going to naturally occur. By caring for ourselves in this way, we are providing for our vulnerable child-self, who is still alive in our memories, the love, acceptance and nurturing that we needed when we were that child.

Emotions themselves cannot harm us, no matter how intense they may be. As human beings, we are designed to feel. What does the harm is self-rejection, which increases and prolongs the pain. With self-acceptance, the pain is reduced to its proper proportion, efficiently released and healed. Not only that, we are then able to learn and grow as a result of the experience. It is our conscious-awareness that grows, and it is our conscious-awareness, self-sustaining and independent of our primal human minds, that provides a secure environment for our human minds and bodies. With such an empowered awareness, life is no longer a problem, but an opportunity. I will talk more about conscious-awareness in the next chapter.

This awareness is essential for releasing that emotional dam. It is essential for the reprogramming of our minds that can be done once this build-up of emotional pain is released.

Once the more intense emotional pain is released, an increasing awareness of the self-attacking thoughts that drive the pain emerges. As we continue on with our lifestyle of self-acceptance, we learn to hold all thoughts up to the light of the reality that we are worthy of love no matter what. We can then ask ourselves, "Am I loving myself with this thought, or am I attacking myself?" We are soon able to identify a self-attacking thought whenever we feel ourselves caught in emotional pain. As a result of this growing awareness, we naturally begin to change the nature of our thoughts. We take more care to treat ourselves with loving kindness. Inevitably we increasingly feel more positive and at peace. The experience of increased self-control, or self-mastery, as it is sometimes called, also arises from this awareness. We can now actively and consciously do something positive about our painful emotions.

This is not some hocus-pocus mystery or magic trick. This is the physics of love. Love heals and brings all things into harmony. Hate, driven by fear and confusion, wounds and destroys. Real unconditional love, however, is no simplistic bit of Hollywood fluff. It requires some real wisdom and dedication to learn how to live it, but live it we can.

Our own emotions are telling us all the time what sort of internal environment we are creating for ourselves. It is here that we discover what we really can control in our lives. Potentially we have complete control over our own minds, regardless of our circumstances and conditions. Any step toward making this personal potential real is a step toward happiness and fulfilment.

By making the practice of self-acceptance our new lifestyle, our emotional pain becomes less scary and more approachable, more understandable. As we continue to observe the confusion within our own minds, we come to realise how much we are hurting ourselves with our own self-attacking thoughts. We realise that we spend so much time obsessing about what we think others are thinking about us—all negative of course, or so we think. In reality, it is our own minds playing out a self-created drama in our own heads, which most often has no basis in reality. We begin to really see the emotional consequences of our own thoughts. This can be an uncomfortable realisation, but when we remember to accept our humanness, we realise that we are not bad, we just get confused and this confusion can be overcome.

It is much easier then to see how to appropriately deal with any negative situation that is still occurring in our lives.

I will go further into the dynamics around emotions and emotional healing when exploring steps 2 and 3.

EXERCISE 2:
BE YOUR OWN LOVING GUARDIAN

Make good use of your journal while doing the exercise. Writing down your thoughts greatly increases the effectiveness of the process. See "5 Keys to Caring for Yourself" on page 77.

Read the exercise through first before you start in order to gain a good feel for the process. Also, make good use of appendix 1 and 2 at the back of this book to help you identify and work with your emotions.

1) What this exercise is about is being the wise, loving parent to your own fragile, vulnerable, confused and often frightened human-self. It is realizing that love is something that we can access internally. We are always within the embrace of universal love and we access this love at any time through actively and responsibly caring for ourselves.

2) Today, right this moment, make a rock solid commitment to treat yourself and speak to yourself only with loving kindness, compassion, forgiveness, and acceptance.

3) Keep a little notebook in your pocket or your handbag that you can use to write down your self-rejecting thoughts as you become aware of them.

4) When you catch yourself thinking this way, in that moment or later on that day or evening when you can make time, focus on that thought and feel into what it does to you. Write down what you discover.

5) When you are aware of this state of self-rejection, imagine this human-self that you are putting down

is you when you were a vulnerable child just wanting to be loved.

6) Be open to whatever emotions that are released during this process. Do your best to let them flow. Acknowledging your own pain works the same as when someone else important to us acknowledges our pain. Suddenly we feel safe to let is out. Let it flow and trust that the emotional release will pass naturally and have a chance to heal in the process. Much of this pent up emotion comes from our childhood. We were so small and powerless then. We tend to feel that way again as the emotions are coming through. This can be uncomfortable at first. Remember that you are an adult now with conscious-awareness. Know that your intentions to care for yourself will help heal this pain.

7) Imagine yourself as that child and think of how you would want to be treated and explore this in your journal. Just let this come in any way it comes. After exploring this, write a note to your adult-self telling your adult-self how you want to be treated.

8) As your adult-self, spend time contemplating the significance of your relationship with your vulnerable human-self, this emotionally wounded child within you. Contemplate the reality of your responsibility toward yourself and the consequences of not taking loving care of yourself.

9) Realise that you did the best you could in the past with the awareness that you had. This also applies to your efforts now. Forgive yourself for your human mistakes and realise that you now have an opportunity to treat yourself differently, and to work toward healing the wounds of the past. Forgiving

yourself is an important step toward living this new way of life. Spend some time writing in your journal about what is coming through for you about this.

10) Contemplate ways to mentor yourself and care for yourself, considering what your inner-child has communicated to you.

11) Let your feelings guide you as you explore this new way of caring for yourself. To help you recognise what is for your highest good, consider these new ways of caring for yourself in the long term. Would it be sustainable? Would it enhance your life in the short, medium and long-term?

12) Don't be concerned about finding the perfect answers. It is all a journey of trial and error. Any step toward genuinely caring for yourself is going to improve your life. Be free and open to learn from each attempt to act more lovingly toward yourself.

13) Write out on a card or in your pocket book your new positive intentions toward yourself and refer to it regularly in order to keep your conscious-awareness active.

14) You can even program your mobile phone to give you this message every couple of hours. Regular reminders are essential for reprogramming the old conditioning.

15) When you catch yourself again in a state of self-rejection, you have these new strategies to fall back on. When you refer to these new positive intentions in that moment, you will have more clarity of the consequences of self-rejection. You will also have more clarity around how to treat yourself with loving kindness in that moment.

16) Continue to put this exercise into practice on a daily basis. Try to see this as your new lifestyle, not some unrealistic quick fix. Recognise that when this is your new lifestyle, you will naturally continue to heal and grow. Happiness and fulfilment are inevitable.

17) In order to empower your healing and personal growth, explore ways that you can reach out for help and support. This is also caring for yourself. Refer to "Five Key to Caring for Yourself" on page 77.

CHAPTER ONE SUMMARY

1. The opposite of self-acceptance is self-rejection, which says we are unworthy because we are human. This is the root of all destructive thought—suffering.
2. Repeated thoughts develop into subconscious beliefs that control our everyday perceptions.
3. A misbelief is any belief that contradicts Unconditional Love.
4. As children we are powerless, vulnerable and dependent on our carers.
5. As vulnerable children we are compelled to believe what our carers repeatedly tell us or demonstrate to us, even when it is not true.
6. What we learn to believe as children becomes our social conditioning.
7. Misbeliefs distort our perceptions of reality, which can cause us to act/react inappropriately throughout our life.
8. When we blindly act out our negative conditioning, without knowing it we are attacking our own self with our own misbeliefs.
9. Self-rejection, whether conscious or unconscious, leaves us vulnerable to the negative judgments and actions of others.
10. Self-rejection, whether conscious or unconscious, can lead us to mistake innocent actions of others for something malicious.
11. Self-rejection, whether conscious or unconscious, can lead us to self-neglect.
12. Self-rejection, whether conscious or unconscious, leads to selfishness—an unhealthy dependency on others and material things.

13. The pressure to perform, to measure up, has become so great in our society that our socially-conditioned minds are stuffed full of self-condemnation about all the little and big ways we do not measure up.

14. Misbeliefs of self-rejection can create a build-up of emotional pain that can lead to destructive behaviour.

15. This back-log of emotional pain needs to be released with care and skilful guidance.

16. Emotions and feelings exist to tell your adult conscious-awareness vital information about the state of your mind, and what is going on around you.

17. To effectively manage your life, you must learn to tune in to your emotions and feelings and understand what they are telling you.

18. It is easier to face our fears and insecurities when we accept our right to be human.

19. Self-care is about having a genuinely loving relationship with yourself.

20. A profound degree of self-acceptance is the key that frees us from suffering.

21. Self-acceptance opens the door of our mind to Love and healing.

22. Self-acceptance is a healthy form of self-love.

23. An adult with a healthy self-esteem can shield his or her self from emotional suffering, or at least quickly recover, regardless of the negativity of the situation.

24. Those with a healthy self-esteem carry a strong belief in their own self-worth.

25. Emotional problems are created and compounded by the mistaken belief that we can only receive love when someone else gives it to us.

26. If love is regarded as a universal force, like light or gravity, then we can begin to look at it very differently.

27. Just as we can put up an umbrella to block out the rays of the sun, we have unconsciously constructed a mental umbrella that blocks out the vital life-force of love.

28. We don't really know about love with any real clarity until we can truly love ourselves.

29. Our love isn't actually owned by somebody else. We do not have to do anything to qualify for the unconditional universal life-force of love. There is no standard we have to reach.

30. All that we need to do to qualify for this unconditional universal love is to exist!

31. We are worthy of this unconditional love always. We always have been worthy of this love and we always will be, no matter what mistakes we make, no matter what anyone else says to us or does to us or thinks about us.

32. Making mistakes is a natural part of being human.

33. With self-care, healing and growth are inevitable, along with maturity and wisdom.

34. We can't control how others love us, but we can take charge of how we love and care for ourselves.

35. Start by setting a sincere intention to be a loving guardian to your own human-self and be willing to learn as you go.

36. This healthy self-love provides us with an inner-peace and openness that makes forming loving and healthy relationships with others a natural outcome.

37. If we conclude that we are a victim, then we are running ourselves down. We are regarding ourselves as an unworthy, powerless child, rather than an adult who has the ability to take care of his or her self.

38. Self-rejection is the same as self-attack. These self-attacks are often triggered when we feel vulnerable, which results in acute emotional pain.

39. In contrast, when we are practising self-acceptance, we are able to recognize that any thought that is not about loving ourselves unconditionally is confusion and should not be believed.

40. Observe, without judging, how a small child thinks, and you will gain more of an understanding of what is going on in your own subconscious mind when it emotionally reacts.

41. With self-acceptance, we learn to step back enough to see our emotional vulnerability for what it is—a scared, confused child calling out for help.

42. By staying open to and present with this inner-child, our vulnerable human emotions, with self-acceptance and compassion, the blocked up emotional pain can be freely and safely released. It is easier to let the pain naturally flow and then let it go.

43. Emotions themselves cannot harm us, no matter how intense they may be. As human beings, we are designed to feel. What does the harm is self-rejection, which increases and prolongs the pain.

44. As we continue our lifestyle of self-acceptance, we learn to hold all thoughts up to the light of the reality that we are worthy of love no matter what.

45. When we remember to accept our humanness, we realise that we are not bad, we just get confused and this confusion can be overcome.

46. Potentially we have complete control over our own minds, regardless of our circumstances and conditions. Any step toward making this personal potential real, is a step toward happiness and fulfilment.

AWAKENING YOUR POTENTIAL FOR HEALING AND POSITIVE CHANGE

SELF-AWARENESS

Self-care is essential to our wellbeing. Truly accepting our humanness—accepting that we are still worthy even while we are being human, even while we are still growing up as an adult, is essential for being motivated toward self-care. We are unlikely to be motivated toward this healthy self-care while we are busy rejecting ourselves. Self-care is about having an active, loving relationship with ourselves, particularly if we need to change some deeply-ingrained misbeliefs. We can hardly have a healthy relationship with someone we resent. We can hardly have a healthy relationship with someone else when we resent ourselves.

To have a relationship with someone also means we make the time to get to know them intimately. This also applies to our relationship with ourselves. Do you know your own mind? Being faced with an emotional crisis soon reveals how unfamiliar we are with ourselves.

In my many years of dealing with my own life problems and helping others with theirs, it has become clear to me that there is a higher, immensely powerful and yet seemingly intangible or mysterious quality to the human being and this is our "consciousness". To put it simply, consciousness enables a human being to observe him or herself—to be self-aware in other words. If utilized properly, consciousness has vast, perhaps unlimited, potential for positive improvement in our lives.

Unfortunately, due to our lack of self-awareness, much of the potential of consciousness tends to lie dormant, buried underneath our conditioning, our confused and habitual thought patterns. Much of the time we are not consciously managing our lives, we are instead unconsciously following our past conditioning, which is all too often *not* the best way to respond to the circumstances in our lives now.

In order to access this potential of consciousness, we must wake it up out of its dormant state. There are real negative consequences to living without our consciousness being awake and actively fulfilling the roll of the aware manager of our lives. Many of them I have already mentioned. Without an awake and aware consciousness in charge, our minds are like a house full of children who are frequently left alone to look after themselves without proper supervision. The children may get by in one way or another, but their knowledge is limited, and they are at the mercy of their uncontrolled fearful emotions. These unsupervised children often get in a muddle and make unwise decisions that adversely affect their lives. This is what it is like having our unconscious conditioning running our lives.

RUNNING ON EGO

When we are living our lives in this unconscious way, it is referred to as running on "ego". Ego is our potential for consciousness that tries to manage our human-selves and therefore our lives, but it is limited because of being captured by childhood conditioning and at the mercy of our primal fight-or-flight instincts. Ego is the child, left to fend for itself. As a result, it is a poor manager.

Ego has little capacity to take care of our emotions. Ego is always in a state of emotional vulnerability, even when it is in a dominant position over others. If it is not fighting or running away, it is denying that anything is happening at all. As a result of its limitations, ego is prone to becoming emotionally dependent on other people, places and things. There is little connection to an inner source of love and security. The ego looks to the external world for all its security and fulfilment and gets caught in a dilemma as a result.

Ultimately we are all looking for love. This is the deepest instinct we have. We are not just looking for any old love. We are looking for *Unconditional Love*. To be unconditional, love must be a constant, unchanging force. The dilemma for the ego lies in the fact that everything in this world is in a state of change, even our own bodies. When we lean on this world too heavily, including the people in it, demanding that it be predicable according to our personal expectations, sooner or later what we are learning on will shift unexpectedly, and we will fall down and suffer emotionally.

The nature of ego leaves us with no option but to keep trying to fearfully cling onto this world to feel emotionally secure. In order to survive, we try not to think about the ever-changing realities of life, or we actively try to fight against them. Life, however, is bigger than our ego. When it is time for life to shift, there is little our egos can do about it.

It is useful to regard our lives as a dance and Life itself as our master dance teacher. Every day Life is inviting us to dance with it and learn the dance. In its childish foolishness, the ego thinks that it knows what the dance is all about, and it tries to lead the teacher in the dance. As a result, the ego gets its feet trodden on. Instead of trusting that the teacher knows what he/she doing, the ego thinks it is being victimised by Life, the master teacher. The ego has to let go to the teacher and let the teacher lead, but it is afraid.

Much of the time we don't even realise that Life is trying to teach us something. Even when we do see the lesson, we are too caught up in our fear, confusion, and pride to accept the opportunity that the master teacher is offering us. The teacher, where the human mind is concerned, is the Universal Life-Force of Unconditional Love. On this level of comprehension, Life and Love are the same thing.

CONSCIOUS-AWARENESS

Once we wake up our consciousness-awareness, we can become our own wise and loving parent, effectively nurturing and mentoring our "inner-child", our human-self.

When I suggest that we can become our own wise parent to my clients and self-awareness students, a number of questions tend to arise, such as: "How do I become that wise parent?" or "How do I go about parenting myself?"

We achieve this by doing our best to *be* that wise and loving parent to ourselves every day, while being willing to learn all we can from each day's attempt to live this ideal. In other words, we are accepting the validity of unconditional love, while at the same time accepting the reality of our humanness.

As human beings we are not perfect. We do, however, have an amazing potential for love and wisdom that can be free of confusion. This is the potential of consciousness. Even though we are human, these great qualities can become the ideals that we strive toward.

In my experience, unconditional love is the ultimate ideal. It is the most transformative, the most empowering ideal to consciously strive for. It is the journey toward living this ideal in our everyday lives that facilitates inner-healing and personal growth—true wisdom and maturity.

Consciousness is our potential to adapt, learn and grow. Wisdom is what is attained from this learning and growing. The doorway to wisdom is accepting personal responsibility for all that you think, feel, say and do. Being a wise parent to yourself means accepting full responsibility to love yourself unconditionally. This is how to wake up and become your power of conscious-awareness, little by little every day.

In reality, by making this most important commitment to ourselves, we have consciously accepted the challenge and opportunity of being representatives of the Life-Force of Unconditional Love to our own human selves and then to others. Having set forth a commitment to embraced ourselves in this love, it is much easier then to offer this love to others. It is more of an overflow of what we already have. If we don't get love back from others, it's not so bad, because we are already tapping into its source independently. Also, because our commitment is to truly pay attention to our emotions and feelings and to use this ongoing awareness to effectively care for ourselves, we are going to be far wiser and far more skilful when it comes to dealing with inappropriate behaviour from other people. We are less likely to be used and abused by others, but without getting into unnecessary conflict.

Another essential quality of consciousness is that it is always now. Even though it can become obscured by our past conditioning, it is never really bound by the past. It is always the fresh, unlimited potential of now. Therefore, this unlimited potential to learn, combined with the potential of love and wisdom, enables us, as conscious-awareness, to pull ourselves above our more limited human minds, which are a collection of old habits from the past. In other words, we are able to transcend our minds and in the process, observe our minds and act on our minds from the higher perspective of conscious-awareness.

Being ego is like being in a crowded room. The room represents your own mind. All the people in it represent the different qualities, perceptions, and issues that crowd your mind. The ego is stuck in the crowd. It can't clearly see what is going on because it is on the same level as the crowd. The expression, "You can't see the forest for the trees," is referring to this very thing—the ego is lost in the human mind.

Awakening our conscious-awareness is like getting on a platform that enables us to see things clearly. That platform may be a bit shaky at first, and not very tall, but as we grow, the platform, our foundation of consciousness, grows more substantial and we are able to see more clearly.

It does not matter how unskilful you are at being this wise parent. Every day is an opportunity to learn. Unconditionally loving yourself means accepting your mistakes as a natural part of the learning process. Trial and error is the natural way human beings learn and grow.

This learning and growing is put in motion by setting a committed intention to love yourself unconditionally in every way you can every day. You then do your best each day to learn from your experiences of attempting this great endeavour. It also means committing to learning all that you can about this process of self-care and the laws of consciousness on an ongoing basis. If you put this intention, this commitment into action as best you can each day and never give up, even when you lose your way now and then, success is inevitable, and I don't say that lightly. Success is inevitable because you are born with this potential within you. It is a reality of being human.

It is then a matter of doing your best to be this potential consistently each day, regardless of what is going on in your body; regardless of what is going on in your old conditioning; regardless of what is going on in your ego; and regardless of what is going on around you. I call this operating on conscious-awareness.

HUMAN-SELF

The human-self that I have been referring to consists of:

- **Basic Character:** Base Instincts, Emotions/Feelings, Intellect, Will.
- **Inner–Child**

BASIC CHARACTER

Base Instincts refer to the survival needs of the body. These are primal functions that are there to keep the body alive and comfortable and to enable us to survive and to experience fulfilment on a basic level. Such primal survival instincts include: safety, comfort, reproduction and sustenance (need for food and drink). They are naturally self-centred for survival reasons and therefore have a tendency to be unaware of the needs of others when triggered into a state of fight-or-flight.

Emotions/Feelings that reflect our essential need for love and fulfilment. Emotions/Feelings reflect the quality of the experience we are having. Emotions come from our human fears, like an inner-child calling out for help. Feelings come from our higher-consciousness, such as all the qualities of love. Here we experience our interconnectedness with everything within us and around us. Emotion/Feeling is like a sensory energy field that extends far beyond our physical boundaries and is constantly overlapping with other such energy fields. This sensory field, therefore, can be experienced as gross, fearful, and painful emotions at one end of the scale to ecstatic feelings of blissful love on the other end of the scale. Emotion/Feeling is often symbolized as water, because of its flowing, merging, ever-changing nature.

Intellect is our ability to think, such as analysing, planning, imagining and creating. Thinking gives structure, definition, and order to the mind. It takes our mind-stuff and moulds something tangible with it. Our ability to think is an enormously powerful tool, which we need to learn how to use constructively, or face the consequences of our miscreations. Our higher-consciousness offers us another form of thinking that is more of a pure knowing. This is called intuition. We often experience this when our minds stop actively thinking and are instead simply held open in a relaxed meditative state. Many of the greatest scientific discoveries have been made in this way.

Will. Our will is our ability to perceive and identify with an ideal, a goal, a course of action and drive through with that action. It is the potential of power within us. It is a galvanizing force that gives vision and direction to our minds and what we create with our minds.

All these abilities combine together as a dynamic whole. We are a powerhouse of thinking, feeling, acting, and therefore creating, whether we are aware of what we are doing or not.

Each of us has a natural character that expresses these three qualities in different ways. For example, some of us may express ourselves more strongly through our feeling nature. Others of us may display a stronger focus within our intellect, or our capacity for personal power. This may show itself as a strength or a weakness, depending on whether our conscious-awareness is in charge or our ego. For example, as a feeling centred person, if your ego is too much in control, you may have difficulty with fear and worry, and allow others to control you. On the other hand, if you are centred in your conscious-awareness, you may shine in your ability as a people person, who is a good counsellor and manager and who also has good personal boundaries.

Conscious-awareness also gives us the ability to further develop and balance our character. For example, if you are a feeling person, you may need to develop more personal power and mental clarity as a part of strengthening and balancing your character. Your ego, on the other hand, may judge such qualities in others and lose itself in emotionalism and in the process, not gain the opportunity to develop your character further.

Conscious-awareness is the capable manager of our minds and therefore our lives.

INNER-CHILD

Our human-self is often referred to as an inner-child because we often feel vulnerable and uncertain. We are often at the mercy of unresolved, confused and emotionally vulnerable mind-states—belief systems and memories—from childhood up to the present moment that cause us to feel uncertain and insecure, like a child. When we are looking into our minds at our conditioning and our beliefs that were set in place by this conditioning, we are looking into the past, and often into ourselves when we were children. For the mind, growing up is a life-long process. Accepting and embracing our human mind, our inner-child, with the unlimited potential of our consciousness, makes growing up a lot easier. As I mentioned earlier, having an adult body does not mean we have grown up yet. It is more constructive and empowering to see growing up as a process that continues on throughout our lives. Considering the extent of our potential as human beings, every point along our journey of life is an opportunity to become more of what we can be.

The inner-child can also be a term used for the innocent, free, playful, and joyful child within us that is unburdened by fear and insecurity. In many ways, this joyful child is what we are trying to return to through emotional healing and the activation of conscious-awareness. For a child to remain in that joyful, free state, it must be protected by a loving and nurturing environment. Conscious-awareness, centred in love and wisdom, fulfils this essential requirement for the human mind.

BE THE WISE PARENT OF YOUR HUMAN-SELF

It may have occurred to you by now that being consciously aware of your human-self means that as conscious-awareness, you are somehow operating on a different dimension than your human-self. You are not only able to see yourself in perspective, you are also able to consciously engage in an active relationship with yourself. Even when this difference between your human mind and your conscious-awareness is experienced as very subtle, which it usually is, you can still actively take care of your mind with your conscious-awareness. What this means for you is up to you. What is important is that this ability to be your own wise parent is very real and is the doorway to realizing your greater potential.

Despite the ingrained habitual nature of the human mind and the painful emotions that it can generate, you can take charge of your thoughts and feelings and along with this, the direction of your life.

Thinking, feeling and acting are just tools for you to use. In the hands of your primal instinctual-self, or your ego with its limited awareness, these tools are not going to reveal your potential. Conscious-awareness is where your highest ability to master these tools is accessed.

At first your old conditioning and your ego will frequently get the better of you. This is only natural. What you have now though is an awareness of your potential (Unconditional Love and Personal Responsibility) and a process for returning to that awareness over and over again. Each time you do, you will be that much more aware and that much more skilful.

Do not set limits on the power of your consciousness. Do not think you know all there is to know about yourself. You have barely scratched the surface. What I am presenting to you in this book is only an introduction into the possibilities of self-awareness. Nevertheless, if you are caught in suffering and confusion, it is more than enough for you to get on with the marvellous adventure of transforming your life.

CHAPTER TWO SUMMARY

1. So often, the person that we least know is ourselves.
2. In order to find the power to overcome our fear and confusion, we need to gain awareness of our potential as human beings.
3. Through self-observation, we discover that there are different dimensions to the mind and its consciousness that can be readily experienced.
4. Three of these dimensions can be seen as: human-self, ego and conscious-awareness.
5. Our human-self is often referred to as an inner-child. This is because at this level of mind, we are at the mercy of unresolved, confused and emotionally vulnerable mind-states (belief systems and memories). Without conscious-awareness actively taking charge, this level of functioning doesn't get beyond a primal state of survival, even when we achieve a dominant position in society.
6. These mind-states are our negative childhood conditioning that cause us to feel vulnerable, fearful, uncertain, and insecure, like a child. This negative conditioning then causes self-defeating ways of thinking and behaving throughout adulthood until it is healed.
7. When we are looking into our minds at our conditioning, we are looking into the past when we were children.
8. Underneath, and influencing the way we take on our childhood conditioning, is the unique character with which we were born.

9. Our basic character is a combination of feeling, thinking and will, with one of these traits usually dominant.

10. For the mind, growing up is a life-long process. Accepting and embracing our human mind, our inner-child, with the unlimited potential of our consciousness, makes growing up a lot easier.

11. Ego is the potential of consciousness that is not yet awake. Ego is consciousness that is held captive by the primal, survival-orientated human-self. The ego uses our human powers in a very limited fear-based way.

12. The ego tries to be the manager of our minds, our human-selves. It tries to access our potential and get ahead, but often in self-defeating ways.

13. Our survival-self or ego is rooted in fear.

14. Our ego can't see beyond its conditioning.

15. Our ego is prone to blindly reacting due to confused perceptions.

16. The ego is more unconscious than conscious.

17. Ego has little capacity for healing our confusion and emotional woundedness.

18. The ego looks to the external world for all its security and fulfilment and gets caught in a dilemma as a result.

19. Life is bigger than our ego. When it is time for life to shift, there is little the ego can do about it.

20. Every day, Life is inviting us to dance with it and learn the dance. In its childish foolishness, our ego thinks that it knows what the dance is all about, and it tries to lead the teacher in the dance and, as a result, gets trodden on.

21. Consciousness-awareness is our ability to observe our human self, with its fears and confusions, from a higher level of awareness.

22. Conscious-awareness is the open door to our potential. Living from this level of mind ensures that we can adapt, grow, and manage our affairs with increasing ability.

23. Genuine Unconditional Love and Wisdom (gained through personal responsibility) is accessible at this level.

24. Real Love is a supreme Life-Force that is above and beyond the human mind—it is the ultimate quality of consciousness.

25. Love is a universal force that we all can draw on once we become determined to do so.

26. As conscious-awareness, we can gain the power to take care of our human-selves by choosing to identify with the Life-Force of Unconditional Love.

27. The inner-child can also be a term used for the innocent, free, playful, joyful child within us that is unburdened by fear and insecurity.

28. For a child to remain in that joyful, free state, it must be protected by a loving and nurturing environment. Conscious-awareness, centred in love and wisdom, fulfils this essential requirement for the human mind.

29. We identify with Unconditional Love by setting the intention to be Love's representative to our own human-selves.

30. By working consistently to build this new identity, we tap into a potential that is beyond what we have known.

31. Without an awake and aware consciousness in charge, our minds are like a house full of children who are frequently left alone to look after themselves without proper supervision.

32. Ultimately we are all looking for love. This is the deepest instinct we have. We are not just looking for any old love. We are looking for Unconditional Love.

33. As conscious-awareness, we find the power to care for our human-selves.

34. It is normal to be shifting back and forth from blind ego to conscious-awareness while we are growing in awareness.

35. Our conscious-awareness has the power to embrace the woundedness and confusion within our minds and heal it.

36. We access the power of our conscious-awareness and experience its benefits by following the principles of Unconditional Love and Total Personal Responsibility as best we can each day.

37. By building our new identity based on these principles, our conscious-awareness builds a defence against the self-rejection of our negative conditioning.

38. Making a deep, daily commitment to Love ourselves unconditionally is the ultimate form of self-responsibility, which in turn heals and reprograms our minds in life enhancing ways.

CHAPTER 3

STEP TWO
PERSONAL RESPONSIBILITY

Putting step 1, self-acceptance, into practice, frees us from old self-defeating beliefs that stem from self-rejection, and transforms personal responsibility into an act of loving, patient, and ongoing care for ourselves. We are learning to fill up our own hearts from the inside. We don't need to be so dependent on someone else doing it for us. This does not mean we no longer need relationships. What I am referring to is a natural healthy balance of emotional security, which gives us a sense of independence and inner-fulfilment. From this position of inner-balance, it is then much easier to create healthy and harmonious relationships.

Being adults means accepting the responsibility for our own lives. This means accepting full responsibility for everything we think, feel, say and do.

It is essential to stop and take in the full meaning of this statement. It is essential to step back and look squarely at what the human mind does to itself. At least ninety percent of our suffering is caused by our own confusion. In other words, at least ninety percent of our suffering is caused by what we chose to think, whether consciously or unconsciously. This means that a least ninety percent of our own suffering is within our own control. All of this suffering can be wiped away by changing the way we perceive our day-to-day reality, and therefore changing the way we think about our day-to-day reality. All too often we are living in an imaginary world of our own creation. We are all in charge of creating our own heaven or our own hell.

Only ten percent of our suffering is due to circumstances and conditions that are beyond our control. Even then we can overcome this suffering with the power of acceptance and conscious compassionate care of our own minds. So in reality, our suffering is one hundred percent within our own control.

To the degree that we hold other people, places and things responsible for the peace and happiness of our own minds is the degree that we will not have peace and happiness.

Like unconditional love, this level of personal responsibility is realizable, but only from the standpoint of conscious-awareness. Like unconditional love, we accept the validity of this level of responsibility and strive toward it, while accepting that our humanness still has a lot of growing up to do.

Stepping up to this commitment to personal responsibility validates our own potential, our capacity for wisdom. To consider anything less is putting ourselves down, and limiting ourselves. Every day we are faced with situations that we don't yet know how to constructively deal with. It is always very tempting to resort to old patterns of behaviour that, deep down, we know are self-defeating and then look for ways to justify this, but this just means nothing is going to change. To hold to the conviction that there must be a better, higher way, and continue to search for and stay open to that better way gives us the opportunity to find it. The principles of unconditional love and personal responsibility are our guiding light to this better way.

Having awakened our conscious-awareness, we strive to become the wise parent to our own human-self, which is always like a child needing guidance. Loving, patient, ongoing care is what we truly needed as children. This child is still alive within us. None of us had perfect parents and none of us *are* perfect parents. As adults, there is still parenting work left to do on ourselves. This is a fact of life that we all have to deal with. Step 2 is about accepting this responsibility of care for ourselves and acting on it for our highest good and for the good of those around us, and as a result of this commitment, we continue to grow in this essential wisdom.

Step 2 gives us the opportunity to re-examine our attitudes and our tendency to blame others and/or ourselves whenever we feel emotional pain. We can open up to and care for our emotions rather than try to bury them or feel ashamed or angry about them.

PRIDE, SELF-RIGHTEOUSNESS, AND DENIAL

What is called false pride is another symptom of self-rejection. For example, this is what causes us to deny our part in a conflict. False pride creates in us the need to be right and to see the other as wrong in an unrealistic black and white way of perceiving. We need to feel bigger and better because, deep down, we actually feel less than. Often we know when we are indulging in a game of pride, self-righteousness and denial, but nevertheless we seem to get locked into a desperate struggle against our own lack of self-worth, caused by our own self-rejection.

Shame is often the resultant emotion that is caused by our unconscious self-rejection. Pride is a primal survival defensive reaction to the shame that we assume someone else is causing us to feel. We often feel utterly powerless to change this self-destructive dynamic, and at some level of our minds, we are reluctant to change due to the false sense of security and power this pride gives us. Often we are not even aware of this underlying dynamic of self-rejection and pride, which only adds to the seemingly endless confusion.

We all make mistakes. We all have wayward emotions. It is illogical and self-defeating to maintain the pretence that we don't make mistakes. We are human beings, and fallibility is part of our humanness. If we engage in such self-rejection, we then have no choice but to also engage in self-deception, because we can't truthfully be anything other than human beings.

Because of our lack of self-acceptance, we become people who do not practice what we preach and then actively deny this fact. We impose standards on others that we, ourselves, can't live up to, but refuse to admit this to ourselves—standards that were unrealistic in the first place, because they deny the fact that we are human. We become the self-righteous judge of other people's humanness. As I stated before, we have denied our own humanity, and as a result, we deny the humanity in others. Even when our standards appear be higher in some ways than others, our self-righteous makes us, in many ways, an even bigger part of society's problems.

While locked in this pride-filled, self-righteous state of mind, we are unable or unwilling to see that it is our own mind that is the cause of our suffering. We instead obsess on the perceived faults of others, and then accuse them of victimizing us. We become belligerent and argumentative.

Underneath this scary exterior is a sad, vulnerable child, who is too afraid to let down his or her defences.

This walled-up state of mind can be triggered only temporarily, or it can be the main basis of a person's personality. While it is active, pride and self-righteousness is very destructive to all concerned.

THE VICTIM TRAP

The belief that our mental/emotional suffering is caused by other people, places and things keeps us continually trapped into a disempowered outlook on life. Our beliefs and attitudes surrounding emotional pain can be a major stumbling block to the realization that it is our own self-rejection that deprives us of happiness and fulfilment.

We carry in our heads the childish belief that emotional pain shouldn't happen, as if we should be able to make our way through our entire life without getting emotionally wounded. The real problem is we don't know how to take responsible care of our own emotional pain. Often, when I point this out to people, they quickly come back with a statement such as, "What about all those people who are unkind to me? Surely they are the ones who make my life unhappy and stop me from reaching my potential. If it wasn't for them I would be fine!"

Within this emotional pain can be a fear of rejection, for example, which in turn generates anger, or perhaps grief and sadness. In the heat of this pain we unconsciously make the assumption that someone else is causing our pain. After all, they made the unkind statement or committed the unkind act. "How dare you do this to me!" is likely to be our immediate reaction. But is this really what is going on? Do other people really have that much power over us? Does this have to be the case? When things go wrong in our lives, we feel like a victim. Is there another way?

Every time we blame our pain on something or someone outside ourselves, we give the power of our life to whatever we are blaming our pain on. If only I didn't lose my job. If only the interest rates didn't go up. If only I wasn't abused when I was a child. If only my partner would stop saying unkind things to me.

Meanwhile we ignore what we are doing to ourselves with our own minds. We don't realise, or we forget, that our self-worth is in our own hands. Our emotional pain is ultimately caused by our own misbelief that something outside us has the power to reduce our self-worth. We don't realise that we are rejecting ourselves. When our emotional pain is triggered, we get angry at others, thinking that they ultimately caused the pain. We justify our behaviour because of what we think other people are doing to us, and we wonder why we live the powerless life of the victim.

While trapped in this mindset, we don't stop thinking like a victim long enough to realise that everyone else thinks they're a victim as well. So who is the true victim? Who amongst us is the one justified in believing that he or she is the victim? I am talking from an adult perspective here. Being a child puts us in a very different reality.

Many convicted criminals sitting in their jail cells for whatever crimes they may have committed, think they are victims. In Ireland, for example, the Catholics and Protestants, who still carry on the conflict, both think they are the victims. It is the same in the Middle East, between the Israeli and Palestinian communities, as with all ongoing conflict situations. We all think we are victims, and we use this to justify our unkind actions. We are all still thinking and acting like powerless children, as though we don't have access to conscious-awareness. As adults, we do have access to conscious-awareness, and we can use this potential to look after our own minds.

THE QUESTION OF JUSTICE

When we feel hurt by someone, we want justice, whether it is a minor domestic argument or a savage assault. But what is justice and how does it help us to heal and grow?

In reality, emotional healing and personal growth is not dependent on justice. Justice may be an important part of the process, but for healing and growth, it is not ultimately necessary. Justice in this world is often not even possible. It is important that we don't get hung up on the need for justice as a prerequisite to healing.

I sometimes use an analogy in my talks, which helps people see the reality that healing and personal growth do *not* depend on justice. What I do to make my point is ask if I can cause some pain to a volunteer's arm. Let's assume that you are the volunteer. When you give me your arm, I pinch it quite hard to cause you a fair amount of pain. I then sit back down and quiz you about how it felt physically and emotionally to have your arm unexpectedly assaulted. I start with the simple question; "Who hurt your arm?" Often it's assumed I am asking a trick question, but of course it was me who hurt your arm. Then I ask, "Who or what is hurting your arm now?" You then have to concede that your arm is hurting by itself. A group of cells in the arm are now damaged and are sending off pain signals to the brain indicating this damage. It is no good looking to me to fix your arm, even though I caused the damage. The pain and the damage now belong to you, and it is for you to heal.

Of course I must be accountable for my actions as the one who committed the assault, but that has little to do with your healing. In this way, emotional trauma and physical pain are very similar. Our pain is our pain. Our emotional wound is our emotional wound. We are wasting our time looking for someone else to take responsibility for it.

We can certainly go to a healer, counsellor or doctor to help us heal the wound, but this is part of taking responsibility for ourselves. This is part of accepting that our pain is our pain. When the damage is done, the damage is then for us to heal. Why? Because it is our own mind and body, not somebody else's.

It is no different to riding a bike along a wet, dirt road and getting splashed with mud along the way. It is no use getting angry at the road for splashing us with mud. That's life. We get mud on us sometimes. When life splashes some mud on us from time to time, we have the ability to wash it off. We have the ability to clean and heal our own minds. If we deny this natural ability, which human beings have come to do all too often, we stand in a state of perceived helplessness, despairing at the mud.

At times clients express their anger and resentment to me about having to heal all this pain that has been caused by the cruel acts of another, or the unforeseen circumstances of life, such as the sudden death of a loved one, or a threatening illness. This is by no means an easy thing to come to terms with. It is a tough assignment. I know how they feel. I have used up plenty of my own life shaking my fists at the world and the people in it.

To stand stuck in the victim mindset, however, indicates a lack of awareness or acceptance of the natural laws of life, and more specifically, of the power of our own consciousness. If our emotional pain carries on for too long after the problematic event, then the problem lies in our own misbeliefs about ourselves. We are in fact unwittingly holding onto this pain by believing that we are a victim. Only when we deal with this misbelief do we open the door to healing and growth. If we can do this, every misfortune can be turned into an opportunity for greater inner strength and wisdom. There are times when we are unable to fully repair our bodies, but we do have an unlimited capacity to heal our minds, providing we can overcome our misbelief that we are a victim. We *cannot* act as an empowered, conscious-aware adult and think we are a victim at the same time. We have total power over what goes into our minds and how we arrange what is in there. The key is to harness this power of consciousness that is naturally available to us.

This level of taking personal responsibility for our minds is hard for many of us to accept, because our society actively supports our misbelief in our powerlessness by encouraging us to believe we are victims.

When someone robs our house, for example, our minds react in such a way as to treat the event as something personal, as though the thief had something personally against us, which is rarely the case. Even so, we hang onto this belief that we have been personally attacked by the robber and by an unkind world. We then talk to others about it and they share about their dramas in the same way and we all feed off one another, feeling justified in our beliefs. This of course only prolongs our inability to move on with our lives and hampers our ability to effectively face our next challenge.

Even if we are personally attacked, we can still refuse to take it to heart. The other person's actions are still about *their* confusion. It says nothing about our own worthiness. No matter what mistakes we may make, we never deserve to be abused, and we always have the choice to develop the ability to not take that abuse into ourselves. We can't always control the harm that is done to our bodies, but we most certainly can control the harm that may occur to our minds.

JUSTICE VERSUS REVENGE

We gain so much "satisfaction" out of sending someone off to jail. We are so devastated if they escape justice, but we don't stop to think that these attitudes are not just about justice, they are also about revenge. Revenge comes from a mind that thinks it is a victim, which then, as the victim, wants to lash out. Searching for justice in this way actually impedes our healing and personal growth, and often creates more injustice.

Don't get me wrong here. The laws of our society need to be upheld. If you do the crime, you then must face the consequences. Our society couldn't function otherwise. As a part of the process of justice, however, we have a perfect opportunity to help heal the law-breakers' minds. In other words, to help them realise how fundamentally worthy they really are. Some recalcitrant individuals would not respond constructively to this opportunity. Despite this, I know for a fact that most inmates would benefit from a profound dose of self-acceptance and our crime rate would drop accordingly.

Domestic unrest also falls under this same dynamic—the injustice of my husband's unkind words; the injustice of Johnny's unwillingness to mow the lawn straight away; the injustice of Jane's need to take drugs despite my love for her; the injustice of that guy cutting in front of me on the highway; and so it goes on forever.

When we are tied to this type of thinking we don't find healing. In fact we are ensuring that our wounds don't heal, because if they do, we then have fewer excuses for being the victim. This is the story of why the human race suffers. Buddha said emotional attachment is the root of all suffering. He is talking in terms of adult responsibility here, not necessary childhood attachments. In this context, emotional attachment is the same as emotional dependency. When we see ourselves as a victim, we are making someone else responsible for our happiness. We are emotionally dependent on them to change before we can be happy.

Underneath our belief that we are a victim is a belief that we are not truly worthy or capable as human beings—that we are not capable of standing on our own two feet—that we can't even learn to do so. Therefore, what is ultimately causing our suffering is a misjudgement made upon our own self. Personal growth becomes very restricted in the face of such misbeliefs.

We cannot be hurt by unkind words unless we, in some way, believe them. At some level we believe we deserve rejecting. At some level we believe we are fundamentally unworthy. At some level we think we are still a powerless child and like a child, we are waiting around for someone or something else to give us permission to feel worthy of love. When we feel the pain of our own self-rejection that may be triggered accidentally or unkindly by the words or deeds of another, we lash out at that person, and in the process remain unaware of the real cause of our pain. Instead of solving a problem, we are creating a problem.

Empowered people, who accept, love, and respect themselves, seek justice but take total responsibility for their own healing. In fact, empowered people fight for justice far more effectively because of this very reason. This is why empowered people have joy in their lives whether justice has been done or not.

I love the true story of a black woman in the deep south of America whose son was murdered in the worst possible way by three white supremacists. His body was hung outside her home. The three male youths were arrested and during the investigation, one of the murderers was overcome with remorse for what he had done and testified against the other two. For this he was rejected and cast out by his family and peers. Even so, he stuck by his convictions and faced the truth. As part of this process, he directly sought forgiveness from the murdered boy's mother. She not only forgave him, the bond grew so strong between them that she took him in as her own son.

Being empowered in this way enables us to positively work with, adapt to and overcome life's difficult circumstances and conditions. Conscious-awareness can actually grow in the face of injustice. That is how powerful we potentially are.

Where domestic conflict is concerned, if we are truly empowered with self-acceptance and no longer regard ourselves as a victim, we are much more skilful when it comes to accepting our own humanness and the humanness of those around us. We are more comfortable with open and honest communication. We are more likely to spend constructive time getting in touch with our own issues in a given situation. We are more comfortable with giving the other person appropriate time and space to take responsibility also. The other person will have time to get in touch with their own higher knowing, rather than be kept busy trying to get out from under our fear-based reactions.

To no longer see yourself as a victim, no matter what your circumstances are in life, will open up for you a whole new door to reality, which also gives you a greater access to your unlimited potential. It is not necessary to understand what life is all about. The important thing to hold onto at this point is to recognize the self-destructive consequences to thinking that you are a victim. Hold open the door of new possibilities and you will give Life itself, the master dance teacher, the opportunity to teach you a new way.

UNDERSTANDING EMOTIONS

A major part of overcoming suffering is learning to effectively deal with our emotional reactions. Here is a simple framework to help you better understand why we emotionally react in self-defeating ways.

There are two basic levels to experiencing our emotions.

1. Free Emotional Response

Free emotion occurs in the present moment and is simply a natural higher-level sensory perception, not unlike sight, touch and hearing. Our emotions are continually giving us genuine information about our environment and those we encounter. This information helps us know how to appropriately act in any given moment. For example, you may walk too close to the edge a cliff and you feel a wave of fear rush through you. This is your body/mind giving you an appropriate warning signal. Or on a more subtle level, you may feel the presence of anger in the person you are trying to communicate with, and your body/mind feeds you signals that cause you to feel wary. Of course our emotional responses can also be pleasant, such as when we are being shown loving kindness by someone.

Our emotions also tell us what our minds are up to. For example, if our thoughts are negative, we feel pain. If our thoughts arc positive, we feel pleasure. Emotions enable our conscious-awareness, once it is awakened, to keep track of the state of our mind.

2. Trapped Emotional Reaction

This is old emotional energy that has become trapped within our body/minds' memory network. Most of this trapped emotional energy is left over from our childhood when we did not always have the ability or opportunity to resolve situations that were psychologically damaging to us. As a result, we became confused and took on beliefs about ourselves and the world that were not true.

As I mentioned in step 1, the most common dynamic here lies in the fact that children are spontaneously emotional. Emotions dominate the way these young minds think. When children are happy they are overjoyed, and when they are sad it is the end of the world. Children are naturally emotional beings, which docs not change until they are well into puberty and beyond when their rational minds start to get a grip, for better or for worse, on their emotions.

Unfortunately, evolving into adulthood means that we are liable to forget what it was like to be a child. We seldom have patience for children who cannot act like adults no matter how hard they try. When children are judged and rejected for being emotional, for not being able to control their needs or emotional reactions, it puts them in an impossible bind. They desperately need our love, but they can't stop being children without having to endure the wrath of confused carers. As a result, as children, we learn that emotions are a problem that should be gotten rid of, or if we still can't control our emotions, we learn to be ashamed of them. What we don't learn is how to appreciate our emotional nature and how to process our emotions appropriately.

Over the formative years of childhood we may repeatedly encounter these invalidating situations. Often invalidating situations can be subtle and difficult to isolate. An example of this is if the child's natural character or personality is very different to his/her parent's character. As a result, the parents may simply misunderstand the child and keep expecting the child to be like them, trapping the child in an ongoing psychological dilemma.

If these disconnections keep occurring, children invariably develop negative beliefs about themselves and the world. During childhood, these misbeliefs distort our perceptions, which then cause us to mishandle day to day situations. Early on in childhood, therefore, our suffering increasingly becomes self-perpetuating. Emotional woundedness continues to build up within our memories and becomes this monster lurking within our minds, ready to unleash itself the next time we feel emotionally vulnerable.

When these unconscious misbeliefs are carried into adulthood, they are still going to be controlling the way we approach life, and will cause us to react to situations in distorted ways that create pain and conflict. As adults we still hold mistaken beliefs such as we are unworthy for simply being who we are. In our subconscious minds, the conflict with our vulnerable wounded emotions remains. The monster still threatens us.

When a situation naturally triggers a free emotion, similar trapped emotional memories that have built up over time can also be triggered. When this happens, there is a cascade effect where the emotional charges contained within these associated memories are released into our present awareness. This all happens in a split second and most often we don't recall the memories as such. We only feel the sudden emotional impact, which can at times be dramatic. As a result there is an over-reaction—a reaction that simply does not match what is occurring in the moment. Without us even realising it, past emotional trauma floods our minds and distorts our ability to think rationally.

In a split second our minds are wrenched out of the present moment and tossed into a tangled mess of painful memories and distorted perceptions. This distortion of reality is the root of all conflict in our lives, because it distorts the very foundations of what we think is true.

This sudden release of trapped emotional energy, in turn, triggers our primal fight-or-flight reaction, which causes us to be defensive or attacking. We are acting out old emotional memories as though it is all happening again now.

Because these reactions are usually intense, they tend to have a negative impact on whoever triggered them, whether innocently or as a result of doing something inappropriate. The associated person is then triggered and reacts, which only serves to pour petrol on the fire that is already raging within our minds.

When in the grip of fearful trapped emotions, we feel like a desperate, powerless child and an everyday situation suddenly feels like life or death. In our desperation we either want to shut down, run away, or lash out. This reactive state is sometimes referred to as "shadow boxing" or being haunted by the ghosts of our past.

As our conscious-awareness grows, we are able to increasingly recognize the warning signs of trapped emotional energy and know that it is our own mind that has been thrown into a state of confusion. It is difficult at first to catch the reaction in the moment. Usually, once committed to a process of emotional healing and self-awareness, such as I am offering in this book, we are able to realise what has occurred much sooner after the event. It is then a matter of accepting what has happened, forgiving our humanness for negatively reacting and, importantly, spending time looking/feeling into ourselves and caring for that wounded child within. It is within this release of trapped emotional energy that we have an opportunity to reach our inner-child and gain more awareness of the confusion that keeps the wounds alive. The emotional upset becomes an opportunity to heal and grow.

Childhood emotions are intense because, as children, we are acutely vulnerable. This is why traumatic childhood emotional memories are felt so intensely when they flood into our adult minds. Even so, it is important to understand that being an adult, we now have the ability of consciousness-awareness that enables us to hold steady and look directly into the emotion. When we do, we can take care of our own emotional trauma in the same way that we can take care of our own upset children. We take care of our children by providing calm acceptance to their distress. This enables children to move more easily through the pain to a place where they can listen to guidance. We can then talk to our children about what is going on for them. Often the upset is more about their confusion. Sometimes there is something important and real that has to be addressed. In this calm, objective space, the reality of the situation can be uncovered. As a result of not being made wrong for getting confused, children are more relaxed and open to guidance. After a little bit of mentoring and a hug, our children are once again happy and free.

Our own triggered childhood emotions are most often the same. When we can accept and take responsibility for our humanness and look directly into the emotional upset, the confusion that is driving the upset is soon revealed. In the light of our conscious-awareness, and particularly in the light of our personal commitment to love ourselves unconditionally, the old misbeliefs just crumble. The monster wasn't really a monster at all—just a confused and frightened child. The acceptance of our humanness and our compassionate intension to take responsible and loving care of it is the key. Regardless of how unskilful we are at this process of caring for our emotions, or our own children for that matter, our sincere intention to put into practice steps 1 and 2 of the 5 Step Process helps us to have a different perspective on our problems. This different perspective enables us to learn something more from each experience.

When the emotional release is around a more serious childhood trauma such as dangerous neglect, physical violence, or sexual abuse for example, the process is basically the same, except you may require some assistance to work with the fear and pain. The confusions that you are working with are the misbeliefs that you took into your mind that disempower you today. The more you are able to face and dismantle these misbeliefs, the more you are able to believe in yourself. The more you believe in yourself, the more courage and confidence you will have to face and overcome this trauma and take action if and when it is appropriate to seek justice. You are an adult now. You have the power over your own mind and therefore your life. Your absolute, unquestioned worthiness, your oneness with love, with life, is in your hands. You have complete authority over your own being.

As we continue working with this self-caring process, eventually we are able to effectively contain such reactions before they start lashing out at others or ourselves. As a result of our ongoing healing process, our conscious embrace of our human mind can become sufficiently developed. There is always something new to learn, however, and there is often a new emotional vulnerability to encounter when faced with a new situation. What is important is developing the skills to work with our reactions, whether at that moment or after the event, and learn and grow in the process. (See step 3 for more on how to do this.)

Like free emotions, trapped emotional reactions can also be pleasant, at least in the short term. These over-reactions can lead to addictions, for example, or falling in love inappropriately. Therefore, trapped emotional reactions tend to be disconcerting because they have a habit of overriding our ability to think rationally and wisely in that moment. We lose touch with reality, in other words.

TAKE OWNERSHIP OF YOUR LIFE

As a result of this confusion, we withdraw our love from those we care about the most, such as our partner and children. In other words, those who we emotionally depend on most are the ones who will most inadvertently trigger our emotional wounds, and in turn, suffer our reactions. We all have trapped emotional energy, and the degree to which it is controlling our minds is the degree to which we cannot function the way we would like.

To compensate, we often avoid situations that we know will trigger us. If the trapped emotional energy is too great, we may end up living in a state of avoidance and therefore not really live. It is usually not until we become so trapped into a situation that we can't avoid that, in desperation, we enter into a healing and self-awareness process. Once we are in this process, it is important to see the opportunity in front of us. If we persist, we can grow to the point of being confident to handle anything that comes our way.

As I mentioned before, we also try to compensate for our lack of love for ourselves by finding someone else to fill that void, which creates a whole set of problems in itself. This does not lead to a healthy relationship, because we are expecting our partner to fill an emotional void that only we can fill for ourselves. Because we lack love for ourselves, we end up needing more from others than they can give. Often they feel pressured and suffocated, and as a result, withdraw from us. Often we push people away because we are afraid we won't get the love that we think we need so much from others.

It is this pressurised, trapped emotional energy that needs to be appropriately released and healed. The mental confusion that keeps perpetuating this emotional energy needs healing or "re-parenting" through wise counselling and in-depth therapy and/or our own ongoing emotional processing. Our misbeliefs about our fundamental worthiness keep negative life patterns going round and round. We must learn how to turn off the mistaken belief that we are unworthy of love on this deep fundamental level and replace this confusion with ongoing loving acceptance of ourselves.

When we have given ourselves this essential gift of unconditional love consistently enough, it then naturally and easily flows on to others. Therefore, every adult has a responsibility of care toward their own emotional wounds. What we need is faith in ourselves, and a sensible willingness to reach out for help when needed.

Personal responsibility is about taking charge of your life and believing in your own unique potential. You are a genuine, priceless, one-of-a-kind gift to this world.

Combining unconditional love with personal responsibility is the key to change—it is the key to overcoming all difficulties in your life. You are responsible for loving yourself unconditionally and you have the power to do it, because you are *in love* all the time, whether you can feel it or not. Just know that you are and act accordingly. Never give up. Success is inevitable!

Steps 3 and 4 are about how to put these principles into action.

On the following pages I have outlined five important keys to caring for yourself.

5 KEYS TO CARING FOR YOURSELF

1. Daily Journal

Keeping a daily journal is the cornerstone to caring for ourselves. Finding the discipline to keep a daily journal can be difficult at first. Our initial resistance is a good indication as to how much we have learned to habitually tune out from ourselves. We habitually look for love outside of us. We are looking for someone else to take responsibility for us. Sitting down at our journal each day is like sitting down over coffee, as the conscious self, with our friend, our human self. If we resent our friend, we are not going to be motivated to spend time with him/her. When we are caught up in victim thinking, the wounded inner-child, who still lives inside our minds, is running the show. Our inner-child is always looking for someone else to take over the responsibility of caring for it. This is as it should be if we are a child. However, now that we are adults, such thinking is self-destructive. The adult in us must now learn to lovingly care for our own inner-child. Personal responsibility is about caring for ourselves.

Emotional energy must not be allowed to remain stuck in our body/mind. This brings down our psychological and physical health. If this blockage does occur then the emotions are being held their by confused thinking.

Writing out your issues, feelings and thoughts with the 5 Step Process in mind will enable you to uncover the confusion and clear the emotional backlog. You will learn about yourself and build stronger pathways between your conscious-self and human-self in the process.

Your life is your business and you are the manager. It is your responsibility to ensure that you don't end up emotionally and spiritually bankrupt. Love, harmony and abundance are already yours. The doorway to all this is within the heart of you. Putting your conscious-awareness into action is the key. Your daily conscious connection with your human self is the foundation, the rock that your entire life is built on.

Writing in a journal is about:

- ♦ Getting to know yourself.
- ♦ An opportunity to plan your day.
- ♦ An opportunity to express, get in touch with, and define your emotions.
- ♦ Keeping track of emotional issues that tend to build up and interfere with your peace of mind and wellbeing.
- ♦ An opportunity to explore ways of taking care of these emotions.
- ♦ Uncovering and challenging self-defeating beliefs/ perceptions and negative self-talk.
- ♦ Setting goals and assessing your progress each day without negative judgment.

♦ Getting in touch with your Wisdom by simply endeavouring to take responsibility for the challenges in your life. This can come in the form of:
   o Reminding yourself of the principles of lovingly caring for yourself.
   o Letting go of your need to blame or judge people and situations as wrong, and instead focus on what your needs are and how to initiate action to take care of them.
   o Contemplating on the solutions rather than dwelling on what you perceive are the problems.

This is your own personal workbook. No one is going to mark it. You don't have to write things that are profound— we often do when we don't mean to. It is about keeping a focus on your personal growth—keeping yourself pointed consistently in the right direction. It is particularly about self–acceptance and personal responsibility. If you persist, in a short time, writing in your journal will become a treasured and routine part of the day. It is also a good reality check, because neglecting your journal is a sure indication that you are neglecting yourself. Keeping a journal is a way of getting comfortable with yourself and once you are settled into the routine, it only takes a couple of pages a day to stay in touch.

When you can consistently accept yourself as you are, and keep a daily focus on your life, you can, one day at a time, make great changes in your life.

Meditation
Meditation is also an important part of this process. Meditation is about practicing being present and tuned

into ourselves as a detached, consciously aware observer. Even as our conditioned survival minds keep on reacting, meditation helps us to be the peaceful observer of those reactions, and in the process, heal those reactions. It is a powerful tool for learning to see reality as it is, beyond old distorted conditioning. Meditation enables us to know ourselves, accept ourselves and work positively with what we find.

If you combine meditation with journaling and reading (which can all be seen as a part of meditation), you have for yourself a powerful process that will effectively reprogram your mind and change your life.

There are four main forms of meditation: relaxation, concentration, awareness and healing. **Relaxation meditation** is for letting go of tension and replenishing energy. **Concentration meditation** is for strengthening your will/discipline and for transcending the lower mind, which is essential for building a solid foundation for our conscious-awareness. **Awareness or insight meditation** is for developing clarity so as to increase our ability to work directly with our human-selves and to also more deeply connect to our Higher-Selves. **Healing meditation** focuses on channelling healing energy to the body and mind. An ongoing meditation practice tends to become a combination of these four forms.

Also, meditation is not just about sitting for extended periods of time. The practice of meditation should lead to an ongoing state of what is Buddhism calls "mindfulness", where you are able to effectively tune into yourself at any time, even in the midst of activity, as a process of maintaining a state of conscious-awareness. In fact, mindfulness and conscious-awareness is really the same thing. See the headings, "Clarity" and "Controlling the Breath", on pages 111–112 for more insights about meditation.

There are many good books and CDs about meditation available today. There are also many good meditation teachers who offer courses and ongoing groups.

Be wary of any teachers or meditation doctrines that claim that their meditation technique is the best and only way. There is no one type of meditation that suits everyone. It is better to learn from various techniques and philosophies and develop your own meditation "tool kit" based on, but not necessarily limited to, the four forms of meditation that I have already mentioned.

2. Education and Inspiration

Studying self-care and self-empowerment books is essential to our personal growth and wellbeing. Look at this statement carefully. Note how I used the word "study" and not just "read." When we study something we read it more than once and even make our own notes. It is of little use to read a self-help book like a novel and then expect it to make a difference to our lives. We must study such books, do the exercises and endeavour to put them into practice. If we do this, the same book will reveal more and more to us each time we re-read it. This is how we learn anything. The same goes for self-help audio and audio-visual materials. This is the only sure way to reprogram our minds—to kick out those old self-defeating mindsets that keep blocking us from love, serenity, joy, and abundance.

It is also important to make a distinction between "self-care" and "self-empowerment" educational material. We need to learn how to take care of our inner-selves—our emotions and state of mind—by studying self-care books. We also need to learn how to effectively act and create in the world and to stay motivated, and we do this by studying self-empowerment books.

Few of us stop to think that being inspired is our own responsibility, but accepting this responsibility may mean making the effort to find that person who has the right message for us, and the message we need to hear naturally changes as we change. It is all part of keeping our consciousness focused in the right direction.

Persistent, consistent, focused thought inevitably manifests that thought into physical reality. Your unconscious mind or lower-self is doing this for you all the time, but it often creates what you, as the conscious self, don't want. Learn to create consciously and you will have what you do want.

3. Counselling/Therapy/Life-Coaching

A counselling therapist, such as a psychotherapist or psychologist, is someone who is trained in various processes that help us to get in touch with our issues and find ways of overcoming them. They can help us see our issues from new perspectives and can also help us to safely and effectively release and heal any emotional pain that we may be carrying. A therapist's ability to help us and relate to us is enhanced if he/she is also dedicated to his/her own personal development journey.

We are not failing by not being able to do it alone. What prevents us from seeking counselling is often our lack of self-worth. We feel this lack of self-worth in the form of shame. Shame is a very uncomfortable emotion to feel and we cope with this by covering it up with pride. Pride says we have to pretend we are okay when we know that we are really hurting. Pride was created by being expected, as a child, to get things right first time, instead of being able to discover life and ourselves through trial and error, which is the healthy and normal way to learn. We were expected to do the impossible. Pride prevents us from getting the care that we need. Allowing ourselves to stay trapped in negative emotions and self-defeating beliefs is very damaging to our wellbeing. It is literally toxic to our minds and bodies. Our perceived lack of self-worth is something that we have learned over time. It is a confusion in the mind that can be healed.

We are all limited by our personal experiences and our beliefs. Every athlete who wants to reach a high standard needs a coach. We need to interact with someone who is trained in mental/emotional "fitness" to give us new information and a new perspective. Conscious Living is a skill like anything else, and this skill needs to be learned in order to gain the fulfilment we are looking for. There is no-one who would not benefit from working with a personal Counsellor/life-coach, and most highly-successful people do just that.

4. Self-Awareness Groups

Another way our fear traps us into self-destructive cycles is when we believe our mind when it says not to trust anyone. I often hear the statement, "I don't trust anyone I don't know." How then are we going to get to know anyone new? How are we going to learn anything new? We also want people to be perfect in some way that suits our own particular comfort zone before we trust them. Such fears can only be overcome by learning to trust ourselves to know how to work with any new situation. We can always think of instances when people have hurt us, but when we think of these instances, we don't take the next step and look at how we got ourselves into these situations in the first place.

Also, the quality of our relationships reflects the quality of our relationship with ourselves. Once again it is time to stop being the victim and start taking care of ourselves.

It is not what happens to us, it is how we feel about it and deal with it that determines the quality of our experiences. Finding a self-awareness group to participate in enables us to be in a group of like-minded people who are making the effort to accept themselves and one another. When we make the effort to regularly attend such a group, we quickly realise that we are not so different after all, that their stories are very similar to our own. We get to hear how they are putting the principles of personal care and self-empowerment to work in their lives and therefore learn from their experiences. We begin to feel more comfortable about ourselves through the loving acceptance of the others in the group and we link up with people who truly know how to care about us, because they are making the effort to care about themselves. We are nurturing ourselves by linking up to a caring community of positive people.

Participating on a weekly basis in such a group is one of the best ways of finding self-acceptance and the life-skills that you are looking for, which is essential for opening up to our own higher wisdom.

5. Look After Your Body

Another obvious tell-tale sign that we are not caring for ourselves is the way we take care of our bodies. I am not going to talk at length about healthy diet and fitness. We all know what this means, and there are countless books on the market that can guide us in this area. As always, common sense is the key.

Consciously caring for ourselves includes going for regular walks, for example, and making the time to prepare wholesome meals. Neglecting our physical fitness, under-eating or over-eating, rigid and obsessive diets or frequently eating poor quality foods means that we need to accept and love ourselves more.

Rest and Recreation

We need to make a distinction between rest and recreation. Rest is about the cessation of activity. A round of golf is not rest, it is recreation. Rest is essential for healing and rejuvenation of body and mind. Rest in the form of meditation is one of the best ways to learn how to relax. Relaxation meditation is very easy to do. It is now very commonplace, so finding a suitable meditation tape/CD or someone to show you some simple techniques takes little effort. Just sitting on a grassy slope looking out over a lake is a relaxation meditation. Some forms of Yoga fit into this category as well. If you can't sit still for any length of time then you need to get in touch with why, because if you don't, you are liable to have a very short life.

Meditation is also about having a restful mind. We can have a restful mind while being active, and indeed this is the goal one would wish to achieve. A restful mind is a mind that has clarity, joy and detachment. Usually we have to start this practice sitting down and doing it in a more concentrated form before we are then able to take it into our daily activities, in the form of the mindfulness that I mentioned before. The 5 Step Process that you are beginning to learn by reading this book is a powerful meditation that we can take with us wherever we go.

Having fun in the form of recreation is also essential for healing and rejuvenation. All too often we get on the treadmill of thinking that we can't be happy until we achieve this or that, or until a certain person treats us "properly".

Meanwhile we are wasting our opportunity to enjoy life now. Happiness is a choice. It does not depend so much on outside circumstances. We can literally choose to have fun whenever we wish, and this is essential for inner-healing and personal growth. Our body and mind need to rest and find enjoyment in order to have time to fully integrate our lessons in life and the expansion of consciousness this causes. We need to realise that when our minds change, our bodies changes as well. The atomic structure of our bodies is actually going through an evolutionary process. This refinement of the body is driven by the evolution of our consciousness—personal growth in other words. Our bodies are denser and naturally takes longer than the mind to settle into the new ways of perceiving life.

If we don't make the time to rest and have fun, we soon lose our motivation and vitality, and we may even burn out. Like a restful mind, a joyful mind is a clear mind. A clear mind is a creative mind—one that looks for solutions rather than worries about problems. Furthermore, once you have connected up to your self-awareness group, there is a good chance you will find someone to share fun times with and with whom you can also relate.

EXERCISE 3:
SEPARATING FACT FROM FICTION

Our human minds have an amazing ability to create their own imagined reality and then transpose that imagined reality onto actual reality to the point of not knowing the difference. We do this by adding imagined information to the actual information that we are taking in about a real event. Here is a hypothetical example: you may make an innocent comment to me about my looks, simply noting something that you find interesting, even praiseworthy. I assume you are putting me down and think that I have to defend myself. As a result, I angrily tell you to mind your own business. To make matters worse, I look at you with suspicion from that moment on.

This misunderstanding occurred because I imagined that you were trying to put me down, when in reality I had no information about the motives behind what you said. Without me being aware of it, my mind imagined a motive and added this to the picture. Furthermore, I held you responsible for what my imagination added. I didn't realise that you had inadvertently triggered a set of painful memories from my childhood. Even though I had mostly buried these memories, my fight–or–flight defences were still on a hair trigger. My primal mind was still trying to protect me in its limited way.

This is something that is happening all the time. We are projecting our own imagination onto the reality in front of us. One of the main reasons our minds do this is for self-protection. In reality though, we are unconsciously trying to protect ourselves from our own painful emotional memories (refer to "Understanding Emotions" on page 69 in this chapter). We have become so used to doing this as a part of our conditioned ways of thinking. We are convinced that what we imagine is real. We are not aware that this added information comes from our own minds and is the product of our own poor relationship with our own selves. We are still believing that we are not worthy in some way. We are trying to protect ourselves from this unconscious thought. It is the confused child within us who is still dominating our thinking.

What makes matters worse is that we tend to be very resistant to looking at this confusion directly, because of how deeply it has become a part of our defence system. We are loath to let go of what we have added to the moment. After all; what if we are right? Unfortunately we are wrong most of the time! This is a major part of the reason why we create our own suffering. This is also one of the major reasons for relationship breakdown. We end up not having a relationship with our chosen partner at all. All we end up seeing and fighting with is our own painful memory-driven imagination that we are projecting onto our chosen partner.

To give you a further example of how the ego's drama play can take over our lives, let's pretend we are in a relationship. I have levels of trauma still active within my mind from childhood that has been further compounded by a poor first relationship choice, which was a symptom of my negative conditioning. I have learnt some lessons from my previous relationship and assume that I have left it all behind me, unaware of how deep the pain and confusion really is. I am confident that my new relationship with you will give me the security and happiness I am looking for. As a result, my heart is open and vulnerable to you, which unconsciously leaves what remains of my past trauma very open to be triggered also. After the glow of the first six months or so of the relationship, my attachment to you, and dependency on you, is deepening. As a symptom of this growing dependency, my expectations of you, that you have little chance of living up to (and probably don't even know about), start to encroach onto the relationship. I may also be under some sort of ongoing stress. This may cause me to unconsciously compensate by emotionally depending even more heavily on my relationship with you to feel secure. As a result, the deeper layers of my past trauma start rising to the surface.

Because you are human, sooner or later you do or say something that triggers my trapped emotional energy, and as a result, my mind is suddenly taken over once again by the drama play of my childhood conditioning. As my passed trauma continues to invade my mind, I increasingly see you from the mindset of the powerless and hurt child within me. As a result of falling out of my fragile conscious-awareness, my mind increasingly regards you as being responsible for my pleasure or pain; my emotional security, in other words. If I am feeling pain, then I will naturally be upset at you for *not* ensuring that I feel pleasure. As time continues on, and if I am unable to take responsibility for my pain and regain my perspective, my fight-or-flight survival mind begins looking at our whole relationship for reasons why I keep feeling this pain. The process of condemning you for not living up to my expectations begins. I have lost touch with my conscious-awareness. I have forgotten that as soon as I am feeling fearful emotions, as soon as I start making myself or you wrong, I am getting lost in the confusion of past negative conditioning.

By perceiving you through the eyes of a powerless and hurt child, I have become dependent on you to change before I can be happy. Worst still, my survival mind now has use of my adult power, so anger and pride in the form of self-righteousness is my safety zone. To feel safe I must be right and you must be wrong. I may try to solve this situation by lashing out at you and pushing you away, while the whole time it is my ghosts of the past that I am fighting, thinking that these ghosts are you. Unless I am able to wake up out of this bad dream and take back conscious control of my vulnerable mind, my relationship with you may tragically come to an unnecessary end.

There are other reasons, a part from **conditioning from painful memories,** that explain why we unconsciously project our imaginations onto the moment and then make negative judgements as a result. Here are two other examples:

Social conditioning: We are all brought up within certain family traditions that do not necessarily apply to other families—even to the people next door, or to the people across the street, or even to our cousins. When we are children, our family unit is our main world and we unconsciously grow up to think that the rest of the world "should" be the same. If we encounter significant differences then we unthinkingly conclude that "they" are a bit strange, or worse.

The same unconscious thinking applies also in larger groups. We regard our country's culture as normal, and the culture of some other countries as weird and therefore inferior.

Character Differences: My strongest character trait may be thinking and therefore I love to analyse things. Your strongest character trait may be feeling and so you love taking care of other people. Another person's strongest character trait may be strength of will and that person loves to challenge his or her self in sport and leadership. As a result, we communicate and relate differently, even within the same family unit. Our natural born character differences can lead to confusion and conflict.

In this context, therefore, if your behaviour is different to what I am used to, according to the conditioned programs in my mind, I judge you as being wrong in some way. All I really know is that your behaviour is different to what I am used to. The rest is what I have added to the moment. I am afraid of your differences and push you away to protect myself. I am afraid you won't meet my needs. In reality, my discomfort has nothing to do with your behaviour. My discomfort is created by my own misguided assumptions about you. I create my own suffering.

In regards to conditioning from painful memories, we are *afraid of our own past*. In contrast, when it comes to social conditioning and character differences, we are *afraid of the unknown*. Either way, it is all about unnecessary self-protection. It is the problem of allowing our primal, survival, blindly conditioned minds that are out of touch with reality to run our lives. To live constructively in reality, we must wake up our conscious-awareness. The following exercise is designed to help us do just that.

Read the whole exercise through before you start, in order to help you gain a better feel for it. Be aware always that there is no perfect way to do any of these exercises. The more you have a go at doing them, the more awareness they will help you gain, and the more skilful you will become in your own process of healing, awareness and growth. Your conscious-awareness is an ongoing process of expansion.

Sorting out the facts
1. Write about in detail in your journal the problem that you want to deal with.
2. Describe what you think and feel about the situation and the people concerned.
3. Now take two separate pieces of paper and place a different heading on each one. On the first piece of paper, place the heading, "Facts". On the second piece of paper place the heading, "Fiction". Now prepare to be absolutely honest with yourself.

4. On the Fact page, read through the notes that you have written about the problem that you want to deal with and list in point form the things that you actually *know* about the situation and the people in it.

5. Be aware that no matter how intuitive we think we are, we cannot read another person's mind—certainly not with any real accuracy. Rarely do we know the full motives behind our own words and actions. Motives are complex and many layered. We cannot truly know what the complex motives are behind what another may say or do. All we can ever do is guess or speculate. This list is about what we actually know. It is not about what we speculate.

6. The only real way to find out about the motives of another's behaviour is to communicate to them. In the process we must be prepared to genuinely listen to them with an open mind and talk things through with them. That way the person in question is given a chance to process their own thoughts and feelings and understand their own behaviour, which they, themselves, may not understand at first.

7. When we do try to talk to the person in question, he/she may not be very receptive. He/she may be evasive or even a bit aggressive. We don't know the reasons behind that either. The person might be afraid to open up because of his/her own inner struggles. Most people, if approached with kindness and patience however, will open up in time. With the right approach, most issues can be worked out.

8. There are a very small percentage of people who are genuinely dishonest and full of malice, who we are

better off avoiding. Such people are soon revealed in this process of communication.

9. The truth is: the vast majority of people do not want to be in conflict with us, any more than we want to be in conflict with them. The unnecessary conflict occurs because we are all just jumping at our own shadows. Learning to skilfully own and manage our own fears and insecurities is what makes the difference.

10. We cannot gain the clarity to approach communication constructively until we can see above our own fears and insecurities.

11. Complete your Fact list and review it a few times to make sure non-factual information has not crept in.

Sorting out the fiction

12. Now, in your Fiction list, write down in point form all the imagined information that you wrote in your journal about the problem. Review the list a few times to make sure you have all the information.

13. Consider what I mentioned before about how the mind is trying to protect itself from past painful memories by projecting imagined information into the moment.

14. Write about each point from this perspective and do your best to identify past conditioning, whether it is painful memories, social conditioning or the way you personally relate from the perspective of your own character type.

15. Write down the insights that come to you.

16. Finish the exercise by exploring better ways to approach this problem where you are not making

other people wrong because of your own fears and insecurities.

17. Make sure that you don't make *yourself* wrong for being human. All these exercises are for the purpose of compassionately caring for your own mind and setting yourself free from suffering.

The next chapter will give you more understanding of how to work with any painful memories that may have surfaced during this exercise. Exercise 4, at the end of the next chapter, will help you to process painful emotions.

CHAPTER THREE SUMMARY

1. To be healthy, well-adjusted and positively motivated, I must accept my personal responsibility to Love myself unconditionally.

2. For many of us, we associate being responsible and disciplined with the controlling and repressive demands of authoritarians.

3. When we were children, we were often condemned for not getting things right.

4. All discipline must serve Love and ultimately lead to greater personal freedom.

5. If approached with self-acceptance and self-care, trial and error can be a fulfilling journey of self-discovery.

6. As children, when we lack a real emotionally intimate connection with our primary carers (including wise disciple), over and above having our material needs provided for, we often grow up still feeling emotionally needy and dependent.

7. Without this vital intimacy in childhood, the development of our conscious-awareness is impaired.

8. Because of our confusion, we expect Unconditional Love from other human beings when they are no better at giving love than we are.

9. The solution to this dilemma is to access our own innate source of Love.

10. Every adult has the potential for conscious-awareness, which enables us, as adults, to access our own internal source of Love.

11. Our children depend on us for this consciously aware Unconditional Love.

12. What this necessary self–Love leads to is a healthy balance of emotional security, which gives us a sense of independence and confidence.
13. With this Love I can take care of my own human-self, the child within me, and have better relationships with others.
14. The child I once was is still alive within me in every emotionally charged memory.
15. As adults, there is still parenting work to do on ourselves.
16. Being conscious–awareness gives me the ability to take responsibility for all that I think, feel, say and do.
17. What is called false pride is another symptom of self-rejection and creates in us the need to be right and to see the other as wrong in an unrealistic black and white way of perceiving.
18. Pride is a primal survival defensive reaction to the shame that we assume someone else is causing us to feel.
19. It is illogical to think that we shouldn't make mistakes, that we shouldn't have wayward emotions. It is equally illogical to maintain the pretence that we don't make mistakes.
20. Underneath false pride is a sad, vulnerable child, who is too afraid to let down his or her defences.
21. While active, pride and self-righteousness are very destructive to all concerned.
22. The belief that our mental/emotional suffering is caused by other people, places and things keeps us continually trapped into a disempowered outlook on life.

23. Our emotional pain is ultimately caused by the misbelief that something outside us has the power to reduce our self-worth. In reality, our self-worth is in our own hands.

24. When we feel hurt by someone, we want justice, whether it is a minor domestic argument or a savage assault.

25. In reality, emotional healing and personal growth is not dependent on justice. Justice may be an important part of the process, but for healing and growth, it is not ultimately necessary, and it is often not possible, and it is important not to get hung up on it.

26. Empowered people, who accept, love, and respect themselves, seek justice but take total responsibility for their own healing. We can still have joy in our lives whether justice has been done or not.

27. To no longer see yourself as a victim, no matter what your circumstances are in life, will open up for you a whole new door to reality, which also gives you a greater access to your unlimited potential.

28. Step 2 reveals the importance of examining our beliefs/attitudes and our tendency to condemn ourselves or others when we feel emotional pain.

29. There are two basic levels to experiencing emotions:

    a) FREE EMOTIONAL RESPONSE, which is the genuine information our natural emotions give us about our internal and external environment in each moment that is congruent with the present moment.

    b) TRAPPED EMOTIONAL REACTION, which is old, distorted emotional energy that has become trapped within our body/minds' memory network, due to carrying misbeliefs in our minds. When triggered, these emotional reactions are out of place with the present moment.

30. Most of this trapped emotional energy is left over from our childhood, when we did not always have the opportunity or ability to resolve situations that were psychologically damaging to us.

31. Being so vulnerable, children often blame themselves for situations that have nothing to do with them.

32. Misbeliefs that trap emotional energy in childhood, carry over into adulthood, further compounding the misbeliefs and accumulating more trapped emotional energy.

33. This confusion causes us to withdraw our love from those we care about the most, such as our partner and our children.

34. It is essential to become aware of how we project our fears and insecurities onto the reality of each moment.

35. Our fight-or-flight, primal, survival minds are misguidedly trying to protect us by using our imagination—convincing us that we "know" things that we cannot truly know.

36. Our minds' habit of projection has to do with our conditioning from painful memories, social conditioning and character differences.

37. In regards to conditioning from painful memories, we are afraid of our own past. In contrast, when it comes to social conditioning and character differences, we are afraid of the unknown.

38. Our misbeliefs keep us trapped in destructive life-patterns.

39. Combining Unconditional Love with Total Personal Responsibility is the key to overcoming all difficulties in my life.

40. As part of my healing process, trapped emotional energy needs to be released in appropriate ways.

41. The mental confusion that keeps trapping this emotional energy needs to be indentified and re-parented through wise counselling and in-depth therapy and/or my own persistent emotional processing.

42. The Five Keys for Caring for Yourself are: 1. Journaling / Meditation. 2. Education and Inspiration. 3. Counselling / Therapy / Life-Coaching. 4. Self-Awareness Groups. 5. Look After Your Body.

43. Personal responsibility is about taking charge of your life and believing in your own unique potential. You are a genuine, priceless, one-of-a-kind gift to this world.

44. Combining unconditional love with personal responsibility is the key to change—it is the key to overcoming all difficulties in your life. You are responsible for loving yourself unconditionally and you have the power to do it, because you are in love all the time, whether you can feel it or not. Just know that you are and act accordingly.

45. Never give up. Success is inevitable!

CHAPTER 4

STEP THREE
LET GO & TUNE IN

A NEW REALITY

Step 3 is about putting steps 1 & 2 into action by staying open and aware of the needs and vulnerabilities of your human-self, as well as tuning in more effectively to your higher-consciousness. Step 3 is about processing your emotions and undoing your mental confusion on an ongoing basis. The benefits of this self-care are an increasing self-awareness and personal balance. Your ability to remain in a state of peace and wellbeing, to have clarity regarding your interaction with others and the way you manage your day-to-day affairs, increases accordingly.

Step 3 is the most important step when it comes to making real, sustainable improvement in our lives. Unfortunately it is the step we most often skip over or do in a half-hearted way. It is the hardest step for us to comprehend, because our egos are built on negative conditioning and confusion. The ego blindly perpetuates the negative conditioning and confusion. This step is about systematically dismantling the very thing the ego is built on, and therefore dismantling the ego itself.

Our egos see the world through the fears and insecurities of our negative childhood conditioning. When running on ego we get lost in our confused imagination that assumes, judges, and blames. We live in a world of shoulds and shouldn'ts, what ifs and what could have beens. When we are not pushing people away, we are clinging onto them and compromising ourselves. We confuse genuine needs for childhood neediness. We build defences around ourselves to try to stay safe and comfortable and we try to control and manipulate others to get what we want. Out of shame, we deny our vulnerabilities and put up a false image of ourselves to people in an attempt to win their approval. As a result, our lives are complicated, disconnected, confused and riddled with conflict. This is our human-self left to fend for itself in this world without the guiding and caring hand of our conscious-awareness, centred in the principles of unconditional love and personal responsibility. This sort of approach to life tends to be driven by our fear-based egos trying to escape from our painful emotions instead of genuinely caring for them. Trying to escape from our emotions is the same as abandoning our own inner-child. We remain powerless to take any real command of our lives and our negative conditioning. Our self-defeating life-patterns continue on beyond our control. Step 3 takes us above and beyond the ego's limited capacity.

Unlike our academic schooling, our social and self-esteem conditioning just occurred without us being very aware of how it happened. This conditioning is the foundation for our relationships with others and our relationship with ourselves.

Similar to our academic schooling, our social and self-esteem conditioning constitutes eighteen long years of comprehensive mental training. Retraining this level of conditioning is like going back to university to study and retrain for a new career. It is essential to accept this reality if we want to change our lives. Unfortunately, when it comes to social and self-esteem re-training, we tend to expect it to happen magically, like it seemed to do during our childhood. We resist and even resent having to systematically apply ourselves to the task, such as with reading, journaling, contemplating/meditating and working with a mentor/ counsellor. It is like we expect to gain a university degree by taking a short six-week course that doesn't even involve putting pen to paper. Then we get upset that negative life-patterns still continue. With this unrealistic attitude, we are still in the grip of our blind egos.

When we accept the validity of steps 1 and 2, taking personal responsibility to love ourselves unconditionally, and make this approach to life our way of life, a new reality opens up before us.

We open the door to this new reality by accepting ourselves as we are. We recognise that, like a child, we are always learning and growing and that is only natural. This enables us to open our heart to our own human confusions, vulnerabilities, fears and insecurities. We see that we are worthy of love no matter how human we are. Unconditional love is unconditional. This new and profound understanding releases us enough from shame and the suffocating pride that it triggers, enabling us to enter into a real caring relationship with our own self, even if this is unsteady at times.

We also recognise that we are no longer children; we are adults with the capacity of conscious-awareness. We recognise that it is our personal responsibility to awaken this natural adult potential within us so that we can emotionally stand on our own two feet. The key to taking command or our lives is firmly within our hands. We realise that we are worth the effort.

In effect, we are learning to be our own wise and loving parent, who enables our human-self to continue the natural process of learning and growing. By wholeheartedly taking this step, we enter into the flow of life in a real way and in a way, we regain the zest of our childhood. Life becomes fresh again. Every day, despite its hardships and disappointments, is a new and exciting day. Every day we start again on the process, regardless of how we did the previous day. There is no giving up. Why should we give up? When we have a go every day as best we can, success is inevitable.

In reality, all that we are ever really experiencing in life is our own self. All that we experience reaches our awareness through our own minds. If we don't know our own minds, we can't tell the difference between the reality of what is happening now, right in front of us and the confusions of our own childhood conditioning. Much of the time, our bodies are here, but our minds are somewhere else. We are living out an illusion instead of engaging directly with reality. Step 3, Let Go and Tune In, enables us to take care of our minds while being present with reality.

Some may say that reality is not necessarily a good place to be. It is said the world is mean and tough and out to get us. This certainly can be our experience of the world from time to time. The world, however, is also full of love and beauty. The way we interact with the world has a great deal to do with which side of the world we attract to us. It is fair to say that when we consistently offer others acceptance, honesty, and kindness while also honouring ourselves, this is what we will consistently get back. It is also fair to say that when we are actively healing the confusions within our own minds that undermine us, we will be able to look after ourselves better and make wiser decisions for ourselves on a daily basis. We are naturally going to reap more of what life has to offer. Reality, in other words, is full of goodness and we access that goodness by being good to ourselves in a way that also honours those around us.

LETTING GO

Before we can effectively connect to our wounded and vulnerable human-selves with Unconditional Love, we must learn to let go of what prevents this vital connection occurring.

Because we are in conflict with ourselves, we continually fall into judging ourselves or others. We have become our own worst enemy. Little wonder we spend our lives running away from ourselves. To get away from ourselves, we remain in a constant state of "tuning out". We tune out because we are still stuck in that impossible childhood bind. We think we have to live up to some crazy standard that says we are not allowed to be human while at the same time not being able to be anything else. In order to deny our own humanness, we phase out, and we do it in countless different ways, and in ways that have become so ingrained into our society that we call it normal behaviour. Smoking and drinking are just two ways. There are also many natural human behaviours that are used in distorted ways to hide from ourselves, such as unhealthy eating, work, sex, power, and entertainment.

When we indulge in condemnation, blame and rejection—hate in other words—we ensure that our egos remain the blind play-things of the distorted and heartless misbeliefs and motivations of out-of-control fight-or-flight minds. Instead of facing and overcoming our fears, we are indulging them and perpetuating them. Where there is hate, love is choked out. This includes the way we treat ourselves. Healing and growth are not possible. We remain at war with our own humanness and the humanness of others and at odds with our Higher-Selves. We are inadequately dealing with our fears and insecurities through our primitive fight-or-flight instincts, instead of effectively managing our lives with our conscious-awareness. In order to heal and grow, we must let go of the blame games and accept and comprehend the meaning of step 2, Personal Responsibility.

It is important to note that suspending negative judgment, with its blame and rejection, does not negate wise discernment, a positive form of judgment, which is essential for responsible choice-making. Here we are making choices based on loving and respecting ourselves. Such choices are not about punishing or manipulating others, even if it means we have to say no to someone.

Our blind egos think that judging, blaming, and manipulating makes us powerful, but in fact the opposite is true. We think we are protecting ourselves from hurt, but all we are doing is creating more hurt. It is worth repeating that we are holding those we hate, even in subtle ways, responsible for our happiness. This means that we are forever dependent on them to change before we can be happy. If we insist on hanging onto this attitude, we have rendered ourselves forever powerless to take charge of our own lives, regardless of what is going on around us. Our minds have become full of misbeliefs that create attitudes and perceptions that in turn cause us to be out of step with life and out of tune with our core authentic self. That is why we hurt.

Through emotional pain, our body/minds are trying to bring this imbalance to our attention so that we can consciously do something about it. Instead of recognising that our emotional pain is a call to our conscious-awareness for help, we have learned to shoot the messenger by judging, blaming and rejecting our emotions.

The same goes with our relationships with others. Because we are rejecting our own emotional vulnerabilities, we hate the person who triggers them. Here is another important statement to think about.

Even though these self-defeating mindsets are clearly hurting us, it is difficult to let them go, because they are all we know at first. They were originally formed by a child's mind in a limited attempt to make sense of a world that loves conditionally, which, ultimately, is not love at all. Our survival minds still assume that we need these misbeliefs for protection and to get our needs met. We, as conscious adults, need to replace these old self-defeating beliefs with ones that are more attuned to what will work for us now.

As adults, we are no longer children who are powerless over our own lives, even though we often still feel like it. As adults, we have the power to learn new ways and develop new choices. Life-skills need to be learned just like anything else, but we won't learn anything new if we are not prepared to let go of, or at least question, our old misbeliefs that keep us down—beliefs that cause us to remain powerless victims.

We become lost when we blame the outside world for causing our emotional difficulties, when in truth our difficulties are caused by the way we think about and deal with the outside world. If we don't do that then we assume we must blame and reject ourselves, which is really where it all starts. To move forward we must re-examine steps 1 and 2 and recognise that there is no one to blame. We are not bad, we are just confused and being confused is a natural part of being human. However, if we allow our confusion to rule our lives, then we are not going to change for the better. Step 2 is about facing up to this confusion. Step 3 is about taking this confusion in hand and leading it back to reality.

When we are less inclined to judge ourselves and others for being confused and instead accept our humanness, we are more motivated to own (accept responsibility for) our confusion and do something about it. Only then can we gain a clear vision of the reality of our self and the world around us. Only then will our hearts open enough so genuine healing and growing can begin.

Both action and reaction follow thought. The quality of our lives is determined by the quality of our thoughts. It is essential to realise what we are doing to ourselves with our thoughts, both conscious and subconscious. Even deeper are the beliefs we hold about ourselves and the world around us. These deeply ingrained beliefs determine the way we perceive everything that happens to us. We blindly assume that our particular perception is the truth and stubbornly defend it, no matter what it is doing to us. We don't stop to think that many different meanings can be applied to any given situation, such as the motives behind what someone says to us. So much of step 3 is about letting go of what we think we know and allowing reality to reveal itself as it is.

Often it is not until we really make an effort to let go of judging and blaming and get on with responsibly caring for our own minds in a genuine way that we discover how deeply ingrained our self-defeating beliefs are. We begin to see them as if for the first time.

People who are consistently happy and fulfilled are not simply lucky. Their contentment comes from their willingness to actively take responsibility for their own emotional lives, and in particular, their own sense of worthiness in the world.

Letting go is about no longer believing in hate and condemnation, whether it is toward ourselves or toward others. We recognise that obeying this negative impulse is self-harm. We instead commit our conscious-awareness to the two life-giving principles of Unconditional Love and Personal Responsibility and set about learning how to live our lives based on these principles. Only then can we begin to unravel the confusion within our minds that is the cause of our own suffering.

This is just physics of the mind—the physics of consciousness. Steps 1 and 2 are there because they work, and they work for everyone, and they always will. They are fundamental laws of life where harmony and happiness are concerned.

To find happiness and fulfilment, we must let go of our fear-based need to control and manipulate others in the vain attempt to get our needs met. We must realise that this fear-driven behaviour only leads to conflict. Freedom is an essential, fundamental human need that must be honoured if we hope to find harmony in our lives. We are all the same on this one. We must focus on taking care of our own minds instead. This approach to life inevitably has the best effect on others, because the power of example is the ultimate motivator.

Through our own emotional healing and personal development, we can learn effective communication skills and as a result, we can learn to invite and inspire rather than demand and condemn. We can learn to connect to people's hearts instead of triggering their defences.

When we let go of the blame games, we replace self-defeating behaviour patterns with a focus on paying attention to, in the spirit of self-acceptance and Personal Responsibility, how our own minds react to the world around us. With this new focus, we then open the door to changing what we truly can change, and that is our own minds.

Letting go, therefore, is about no longer holding other people, places and things responsible for our happiness.

TUNING IN

Instead of blindly reacting to, or pushing away, our trapped emotions, we need to be able to stop and observe the painful emotions so that we can know what they are really about. More often than not, they are an indication that a misbelief from negative conditioning has been triggered. Until we are able to look directly into the trapped emotions to where the distorted thinking is embedded, real clarity around our confusion and the problems it causes is unlikely to be found.

Tuning into our emotions and questioning our long-held beliefs is not easy at first. We are shaking up the very things that we thought were our foundations, but if this confusion has been our foundation, we have been living on very shaky ground.

Learning To Feel

To effectively work with and process emotional energy, we need to learn how to *be* with emotions, to open our hearts and minds to them and allow them to freely flow through us. Initially, when we do attempt to work with emotions, we tend to try to "fix" them or analyse them away. This method has only limited success and reaches the problem only on shallow levels. Trying to "fix" emotions is like telling emotionally distraught children to "pull their socks up and get on with it" without actually connecting with them on a heart-to-heart level first. This actually buries the emotion, erodes trust and destroys intimacy.

Neither is it good to pander to the child's emotions, or adult emotions for the same reasons. This just creates weakness and selfish behaviour such as self-pity and self-indulgence at the expense of others. In other words, facing up to our victim thinking and neediness with the knowing that our lives are our own responsibility is essential. A process has a beginning, a middle, and an end. If properly handled, emotions can be effectively and efficiently processed, leading to insight, wisdom and inner-strength. It is essential that your emotional life is respected and properly looked after. Your world will literally come alive as a result.

What needs to be understood is that emotions are meant to be felt. They are like energy waves. If allowed to flow freely the way emotional energy is meant to, it passes quite quickly, once having delivered its message to our consciousness-awareness.

I am not talking here about acting out emotions, like projecting anger onto people, for example. I am talking about allowing emotions to run through our own awareness. Emotions themselves don't really need fixing because that is not where the problem lies. The problem lies with our distorted thinking patterns. It is our distorted thinking patterns that cause, accumulate and perpetuate emotional energy, making emotions a problem rather than a natural and valuable human function. To uncover these self-defeating, unconscious ways of thinking, we need to literally follow the feeling trail. This allows the unconscious to be raised into conscious-awareness, revealing beliefs that are often deeply hidden from normal investigation.

Another difficulty that we encounter when we try to feel into our emotions is the triggering of the defences that our habitual survival minds have, over time, set in place to avoid feeling painful emotions. These defences can be on a hair trigger, and are linked to our primitive fight-or-flight instinct, even if this defensive reaction is subtle.

For example, we may try to feel into an emotion that we want to further investigate, but then it just disappears like a scared animal that has dashed back into the undergrowth of our unconscious mind. Our primal defence systems shut the emotion down. Another subtle mind-defence we can encounter in the process of trying to tune into our emotional pain is when we get the sudden urge to distract ourselves with some sort of activity, healthy or unhealthy. Fear associated with the emotion is the main cause of our subconscious primal need to pull out of the process, even when we are consciously trying to stay with it.

In order to get above the survival mind's primal defences, subtle or obvious, that inadvertently shut out our conscious-awareness, we need to create a diversion, a gap in the reaction, that allows our conscious-awareness to step in and take charge. There are two main tools that can be used to circumvent this fight-or-flight reaction, which are also used throughout the day to stay present in our conscious-awareness. They are *clarity* and *slow, full breathing.*

Clarity: The clarity is about increasing your awareness of how this reactive state of mind feels so that you can effectively identify it, observe it, and take steps to rise above it. This awareness comes from your sincere determination to *want* to face up to and gain command of your self-defeating reactions and in the process, access and activate your real potential.

The essential factors here are firstly, your *willingness* to face your fears and insecurities, which evokes your conscious-awareness and secondly, your *intention* to love yourself unconditionally, which evokes the power of love as a healing life-force through your conscious-awareness. This empowers your conscious-awareness enough to be able to observe the reaction when it comes, or at least do so soon afterwards, rather than be completely swept away by it. With this greater power of observation, your perception of when this reaction is being triggered naturally increases as you gain skill in the process. Eventually you will be able to keep the reaction within your conscious-awareness and dissolve it with clarity and love before it takes control of you and causes harm to yourself or another.

This clarity is also strengthened by the realization that any disturbed emotion is the product of the more primitive fear-based human-self. When such emotions are felt, it is safe to immediately consider that your mind has been thrown into a state of confusion. You must, therefore, stop and check it out rather than blindly act it out.

Our higher awareness can also send us feelings, but this is quite different to basic emotions. Feelings from our higher awareness tend to be more refined, subtle and intuitive and cause no harm to ourselves or others. These feeling can come in the form of peak pleasurable sensations, intuitive hunches that give us guidance, subtle warnings, and much more. Our connection with this higher guidance strengthens as our conscious-awareness develops. In contrast, reactions from the lower human-self are blunt, clumsy and heavy, like they're coming from our inner cave-man.

Controlling the Breath: When the mind is thrown into a state of fight-or-flight, our breath quickens and becomes shallow. Our bodies tighten up like a wound-up spring. Our minds are reduced to a tunnel-vision like state. This is not a state of mind that is going to take the time to calmly assess the reality of a situation. It is a state of mind that shoots first and asks questions later, if at all. It is a state of mind that falls prey to unconscious negative conditioning.

By consciously controlling the breath, you can find the off switch to this blind, primal defensive reaction. You do this by consciously breathing deeply and slowly, with an emphasis on slowly, otherwise you can hyper-ventilate and get a little dizzy. Breathing in this way evokes a state of calm the gently envelops the body and mind. Be aware that this slow, conscious breath is not meant to suppress the emotional reactions. It is instead meant to rechannel them away from the fight-or-flight primal defences and into your conscious-awareness where they can be safely processed.

As you breathe, therefore, open your awareness to your breath. Imagine your breath as a healing, nurturing, cleansing energy that is gently flowing through your heart of awareness from the greater life-force of unconditional love, which it is. Allow anything that you are feeling, pleasurable or painful, to flow freely into your open, calm awareness. Don't try to push emotional pain away with your breath. Let it in and observe it instead, even if it brings tears to your eyes, even if it feels uncomfortable at first. This open, flowing breath is you as conscious-awareness being the guardian to your human-self. It is about letting your higher-consciousness gain access to your human emotions and confusions through your open breath. Your higher-consciousness does the healing work. You are doing your part by opening up and getting out of the way so the natural process of emotional healing can take place. The next passage entitled "The Quest for Healing" further describes this healing process.

This slow, deeper breath is the sort of breath I recommend my students and clients use while meditating, and also as much as possible throughout the day. It is the foundation to practicing yoga on any level.

Breathing this way sends a very different signal to the human-self that is something like, "It's okay. Conscious-awareness has arrived on the scene to take care of things." It is a conscious response that indicates that you are awake, ready, and willing to allow this trapped emotional energy, along with all the mind's defensive reactions and distractions up into your awareness, your heart, and out of harm's way where it can all be effectively processed. As you continue to practice this process of opening your conscious-awareness to your trapped emotional energy, your primal defences gradually give way to your higher consciousness.

This applies whether we manage to catch the emotional reaction in the moment or process it any time after the event, which is more often the case at first.

With this approach to healing, you can know that when an emotional reaction is triggered, it is a call to your conscious-awareness to take a deep breath and pay attention to your own mind. Just a split second pause can make all the difference between an argument and a constructive discussion, for example. Instead of being pulled down into destructive fight-or-flight, this approach enables you to *be* conscious-awareness, observing and compassionately working with your vulnerable human mind and its unconscious reactions.

Don't expect to master this process over night. You are dealing with the human mind here—the most power thing on the face of this planet. You are leaning to master this mind and you will be learning to do this all your life. You are embarking on a life-style change that will enable you to benefit from every experience in your life. Every gain is your increasing freedom from suffering, your increasing peace of mind. Stay focused on the process each day and the results will take care of themselves.

With this new attitude of loving acceptance of our humanness and a firm commitment to care for our emotional reactions, the negative conditioning that causes so much havoc in our lives can be safely re-examined and corrected. Often healing happens quite automatically simply because we are consciously re-entering this vulnerable mind-space with a loving heart. This is something that was missing when we were first experiencing the traumas that became lodged in our emotional memory.

THE QUEST FOR HEALING

Emotional healing is very much like entering through a time-tunnel that leads into various unprocessed memories. Sometimes these old memories resurface quite vividly. Sometimes we only feel the emotions. In a real way we are returning to our memories to where we find our past child, adolescent or adult self stuck in the difficult situation that created the confusion and emotional wounding. This confusion and trapped emotion became buried in our subconscious because there was no one there for us at the time with enough skills to help us process the hurt.

With your new awareness, you are now in a position to heal yourself. You are now that person you need then. For example; imagine a time when you were a child, during a moment of real sadness and intense fear. Imagine being this child feeling lost and alone without a friend in the world. Pause for a moment and allow yourself to return to such a moment in your life. Perhaps you were rejected and tormented by bullies at school. Maybe you remember hiding in your room or under the house after being mistreated again by an adult or a sibling. Perhaps you were experiencing your parents fighting yet again. You feel helpless and hopeless as you withdraw into your shell, thinking that this sadness is never going to end.

Suddenly, from out of nowhere, a gentle, kind and caring person appears before you. You vaguely realise that this person is you, but you as an adult from your future. This older you greets you kindly and then sits down with you. The older you tells you that he/she is now going to be that special person who will be there for you always. Your adult self tells you that you now have a loving guardian who accepts you as you are and who can feel what you feel and who listens and cares about what you need. It feels comforting to be in the presence of the older you but you are still unsure. Trusting someone is still scary. Your new guardian, that is you, your adult self, quietly talks to you about how special you are and comforts you with gentleness and patience. You find that you can open up to this gentle and caring older self and before you know it, your sadness is flowing out in waves of emotion. Your new guardian stays with you and holds you gently and you see a tear of empathy in his/her eye as well, and you feel a warm connection with your guardian. At last you feel like you belong and you nestle into the arms of your loving guardian. When you are ready, you are led into a wondrous place that has opened up before you where you are safe, loved unconditionally and are free to be yourself. You discover that you have a new home.

This is what this healing process is creating for your human-self, your vulnerable inner-child, whenever you consciously stay with and be open to your sad and vulnerable emotions with the desire to accept them and care for them with loving kindness. This child in you is going to have such a different experience. Your trapped emotional energy is going to flow into a very different space within your consciousness where healing is going to be a natural process. The safe and loving home for your vulnerable inner-child is your own heart of consciousness-awareness.

By returning to these past memories in your own mind, with an open, loving heart and a more enlightened attitude, you can literally be there for your own human-self in a way that enables your inner-child (the emotional needs of your human-self) to be freed from confusion and emotional stuckness. It also helps to imagine your aware, conscious, adult-self actually stepping into this scene with your helpless child-self in order to take loving care of this precious child. You have an opportunity to be that special caring person that your child-self has always longed for. You can say the things your child-self longs to hear from that loving guardian, which is you. You can allow your child to perhaps have a good cry, to get out those pent-up emotions within your own imagination and through your own feelings as you hold your heart open to your child, providing acceptance and safety. You can offer the safety, warmth and intimacy that your child-self missed out on. After the initial release of emotion, and once you feel comfortable with one another, you may want to create, in your imagination, a new sanctuary together with your child-self and spend time just having fun doing the things that you always wanted to do as a child. Using your journal is very helpful here, and empowers the process greatly. See Exercise 4 at the end of this chapter.

What you are doing is releasing the emotional pain from the old memory and in the process, creating a whole new positive memory that can now put your mind at rest.

Of course this child is within you and these emotions are going to be felt by you and released through you now, which is often confronting. Staying connected to your slow flowing breath and keeping your compassionate heart open to your humanness enables these emotions to be released safely and effectively.

You may at first experience such emotions as fear, shame and anger. Your inner-defences may block you out of the process for a time. You may even experience you inner-child rejecting you at first. You may, in turn, be tempted to judge your vulnerable self, or others. These are all reflections of past trauma and self-condemnation. As always, self-acceptance and your total commitment to be the loving guardian to your human-self will eventually break down these barriers, as it would have done when you were that child, who is still alive within your mind.

Imagine someone coming to spend time with you, just you, all those years ago and who had all the time in the world for you. Imagine that person not being fazed by your defensiveness and aloofness. This person would just keep showing up, offering you unconditional love. This love would inevitably melt your heart because that is what real love does, if given the chance. There is nothing greater.

When guiding clients through this process, they are often astounded by the vividness of the memories that come through, as well as the new images that are created spontaneously, seemingly from some higher source of consciousness. They can literally experience themselves caring for their child-self, who is independently interacting with them within this mind space, this place of healing. People often have their first experience of real unconditional love during this process and this amazing love comes from within themselves! A whole new world opens up for them.

The process of healing their emotions makes a lot more sense to them after that. It is not so abstract.

The process is usually more intense and vivid when guided by a skilled therapist. Nevertheless, with the use of reading, meditation and your journal and the fact that you have an opportunity to connect with your inner-child/human-self on a daily basis, your own process will have the desired effect. Combining your own process with appropriate therapy will of course empower your process greatly.

It is very important to understand that as an adult, your mind, along with your memories, belongs to *you* now. As conscious-awareness, you are now in charge of this mind space and you now have the power to take control of it and sort it out, no matter how scary the original experiences were. It is all happening on the level of mind, and your mind is within the unlimited power of your conscious-awareness. No one has power over you within your own mind unless, through confusion, you give that power away.

This is valid for both women and men. In general men like to think they are not afraid or hurt. They have been taught to bury their feelings in order to be warriors and workers. Unfortunately this denial of feelings also destroys relationship intimacy. They deny their vulnerability by covering it up with anger, pride and avoidance. Anger is fear projected outwards, which is covering over a vulnerable human-self in need of love. This is a boy who has been deprived of emotional intimacy and shamed and bullied if he tries to enter this space. He quickly loses touch with the fact that it even exists and suffers the emptiness and confusion that men all too often feel. The community then suffers the consequences of this confusion as men try to be dominant to feel safe and think intimacy only involves sex.

I have noticed that unnecessary anger is an increasing problem with women also, who are trying to regain and assert their power. Power must come with love and wisdom. Otherwise it only adds to the problems in our society rather than being part of the solution.

This process of re-accessing our emotional memories is not about self-pity as is often assumed by those who are unwilling to step into this open-hearted, compassionate space. Self-pity is about believing we are a victim, a powerless child. Self-pity stems from self-rejection and gets caught in finding fault. There may be issues that need to be addressed concerning another's behaviour, but until we compassionately deal with our own confusion, we are in danger of approaching these issues as an irrational inner-child rather than an empowered and mature adult. This process, therefore, is about self-responsibility and self-care. You are caring for your human-self, your own mind in other words. You are an adult standing on your own two feet.

The most effective healing for children is to help them know that they are loved, that you accept them and love them no matter what. By giving them permission to safely feel and express their emotions without harming anyone, they quickly move through this energy. They then feel safe and trusting and are ready and open for guidance. Then you can give them a pep-talk and guide them back out into the world again. It is not always that simple, but persistence pays off. The wounded memories in your own mind are no different. The feeling of finally coming home to a safe and loving place of self-acceptance and self-care within your conscious-awareness is no different. You are giving yourself an inner hug.

Our emotional minds are very deep and very complex. If genuine wisdom and maturity is what you want, there are no quick fixes. You are accepting responsibility for your life, as an adult should. Healing one memory often opens the door to another. It is a natural ongoing journey of self-care, mind-maintenance and growing up. Life in this way is a quest for wholeness, a quest to uncover and realise our potential as a human being.

This does not mean we can't be happy and fulfilled until we have reached some far-off goal of personal development. Happiness, peace and fulfilment can be experienced every day through self-acceptance and compassionate self-care. The rest is the journey of self-discovery and increasing self-mastery. This greatest of all journeys is challenging, but it is also exciting, particularly when our persistent efforts inevitably get tangible results.

Being an adult means we must learn to effectively parent the child that is still alive within our memories. One of the wonderful spin-offs of building this type of relationship with ourselves is that everything we learn that helps us to make a real connection with our own vulnerable selves also works where connecting to our loved ones is concerned, especially our intimate partner and our children, which is perfectly logical when you think about it. For many people, making a real heartfelt connection with themselves, and knowing that this connection can be re-experienced on a regular basis, is one of the most special and profound events in their life. This in itself can be life-changing. For those of us who suffer chronic depression, for example, this can be the very thing that breaks the grip of the depression for good, like it did for me.

When our compassionate heart is consciously held open to our trapped emotional energy, once the emotional backlog is cleared a little, space is then available for the intelligence of our higher-consciousness. This is called insight, which reveals a more positive and empowering perspective on any past dilemma. If you persist with this process and make it an integral part of your lifestyle, inevitably your inner-child/human-self will feel loved again and safe again and gain self-worth. Do not underestimate how powerful this process can be.

CONNECTING TO YOUR HIGHER CONSCIOUSNESS

In my experience, confusion sets in when, for whatever reason, we get out of touch with our higher growth-orientated consciousness. When we tune into ourselves and feel, with a heart committed to loving ourselves unconditionally, we are learning to take care of our child-selves, our human-selves. As we are doing this, and at first without even knowing it, we are also tuning into our higher growth consciousness. We are actively shifting our centre of awareness from that of a powerless child to that of a caring and empowered parent. Instead of just acting out our emotional baggage, we are increasingly able to transcend it and observe it, and from this higher perspective, take care of it. In this way, moving into a higher state of consciousness is automatic, because acting on behalf of love aligns us to its source and naturally strengthens this vital connection. If we put in the effort and persistence, we can really feel our inner-wisdom and power coming through, and sooner or later we find ourselves feeling a deep unconditional love that seems to come from nowhere. This is part of that heartfelt connection that I spoke about at the end of the previous passage.

Despite what many people say, you don't have to be special to experience this inner-source of unconditional love. You can have this experience as a normal part of your life. It is as easy as taking the time to lovingly care for yourself, in particular your emotional self, and making this an essential part of your lifestyle. As you pay attention to the task of lovingly caring for yourself, your connection with your higher-consciousness grows as it simply becomes a natural part of what you would call common sense. You are literally *being* this higher consciousness, and therefore you are literally *being* love. Many people have this without even realising it. The rest of us have to make the effort to learn this self-love, but that gives us an important edge in the form of a stronger conscious-awareness. We consciously learn how love works and how to make it work in any situation.

That special feeling of unconditional love, more often than not, just creeps up on us. Occasionally we are able to look back and really see how far we have come, which often surprises us. John Lennon wrote in one of his songs, "Life happens when you are busy doing other things." I would change this around a bit and say that life works for us while we are busy lovingly caring for ourselves, because when we are putting this into practice, we are showing our best side to the world.

EXERCISE 4:
WORKING WITH EMOTIONS

When we are in the middle of a dark cloud of emotional energy, it can be hard to be motivated to do anything. The negative energy restricts our awareness to the point where we just can't see beyond the blackness. In that moment we may have many choices and directions we can take, but our vision is heavily clouded with confusion and emotions like despondency, shame, and anger; perhaps resulting in depression. We may want to lash out at someone, just shut ourselves up in our room, or head for the chocolate cake or beer.

What is usually happening at these times is that a dense layer of painful emotional energy that was previously trapped within our subconscious has now been released into our conscious minds. Perpetuating this emotional energy are old confused and habitual thought-patterns that are laden with self-rejection and as a result, judgement of others. These thoughts invariably tell us that we are not worthy to be loved, that we don't measure up. Our fight-or-flight reaction then tries to defend this misbelieve by judging others, creating even more pain.

There is one thing an adult can do that a child has little power to accomplish, and that is consciously and actively love oneself. We can do this because we have access to conscious-awareness. This may be just speculation for some, but those who have truly put it to the test have discovered the wonderful truth about themselves. Not only that, human beings have been rediscovering this power since the dawn of time, and have left us endless descriptions of their experiences. What is needed is an educated faith that this can be done and a determination to *never give up*. With this universal love it is said that all confusion can be healed. My personal experience of the power of this love is the drive behind writing this book.

No matter how bad the pain, it will end. It can sometimes be like sailing through a very dense fog. We are moving but it doesn't seem like it, because we just keep feeling the same, day after day. The fog seems like it will go on forever, and similarly, our wounded inner-child scares us into thinking that the pain will never end. This prompts our fear-based egos to desperately search for a quick way out, such as with drugs, prescribed or otherwise. But we know medication actually doesn't heal the emotions, and it certainly doesn't empower us with new awareness. Medication may sometimes be needed for a period of time, however, to help us to function enough so that we can start the process of healing.

In the case of emotional pain, the quickest way out of it is through it. The pain is the pain of our own acute self-rejection, reflecting the judgement and mistreatment we may have once endured from others, and may still be enduring. The pain feels all too real, but it is not about the reality of who we truly are.

We need to go into the pain to expose the false image of ourselves and of the outside world that this pain and fear portrays to us. If we run from the pain, we never get a chance to see it for what it is, which just makes its falseness seem more real. As a result, we remain trapped in this distorted reality as effectively as being in a prison. If we face and work with the emotional pain, we gain access to the key to the prison door and the power to dismantle the prison altogether.

Being with our pain is part of the process of caring for our emotions—our wounded inner-child/human-self. It is about learning how to be there for our powerless inner-child, which is so much of what we feel at these times. We all have the power to do this because we all have conscious-awareness that can align itself to the natural laws of consciousness. We do this by learning about and practising self-acceptance and compassionate self-care.

By entering into a process that will raise our awareness of what this pain is really about, the healing power of this awareness will inevitably dissipate the pain, just as the sun evaporates the fog or as a child moves through distress in the arms of a loving parent. Through this process, the choices we have are revealed to us, along with the actions we can take to change ourselves and our circumstances if this is needed. This consciousness-raising process allows the negative energy to keep on moving through and out, and not get buried again in our subconscious. In time the fog will lift, and by entering into a genuine healing process, the fog will lift sooner than later, and we will have gained the inner-strength and flexibility of wisdom and self-love that will be with us always.

An essential part of the healing process is reaching out to someone we can talk to, no matter how much our minds tell us that this will not help, and we need to keep reaching out until we find someone who understands. We need someone to remind us to not be hard on ourselves—that there are choices other than our old destructive behaviour-patterns. We need the perspective of someone who is outside our dark emotional cloud and the confusion that creates this cloud.

Apart from talking to someone, it is always beneficial to express our emotions on paper using the 5 Step process as a guide. Writing out our emotions helps us to really connect with ourselves. We are spending the time to really listen to our wounded inner-child and this expands our awareness of our own story. Putting our emotions and thoughts down on paper helps us to make more sense of them; otherwise these emotional thoughts continue to be a confused and tangled whirl inside our heads.

When we have lost our balance in any situation, this process is always an important step to regaining our centre of gravity. We are refocusing our balance by accepting and caring for our emotions, rather than being lost in them. At first it may seem like it will not make a difference, but this act of personal responsibility automatically activates the power of love and wisdom, whether we feel it or not. Even if it may take weeks or months to make a difference, due to the density of the negative conditioning that we carry, healing is inevitable, so long as we don't give up.

Exercise

I have laid out some steps that may help you with this process. It is best to read the whole exercise to familiarise yourself with it before you begin. It will help to reread the summaries of steps 1, 2 and 3 in order to focus yourself for this exercise. Also, make good use of Appendix 1 and 2 at the back of this book to help you identify your emotions and work with them. This exercise is just a guide. Feel free to be spontaneous as you are working through it. Let your thoughts and feelings flow.

1. Reaching out: If you have a counsellor or mentor, let them know that you are going to explore your emotions and negative conditioning using a step-by-step process. Make arrangements to share this process with them so that they can support you.

2. Opening up: Spend some time writing about the issue or issues that are causing you difficulty. Start by describing the situation so as to get in touch with it.

Pay attention to what you are feeling about the situation and the people involved. Do your best to explore your feelings in your journal. Don't try to be politically correct. Let the pain of your emotions speak freely, without you judging them. Don't forget to use your open breath and the right attitude while letting through these emotions—to compassionately care for yourself and honour yourself.

Remember to keep breathing deeply and slowly with an attitude of loving acceptance of yourself and a desire to responsibly and compassionately care for your vulnerable human self. It is important to allow yourself to feel. Healing is more powerful if you are able to let your emotions flow freely through your awareness.

If the intensity of the emotional energy does get too much to continue the exercise, take time out and perhaps put on some soothing music and be there compassionately for your inner-self. You can stretch out on your bed and surrender your pain to your higher consciousness. Don't try to "fix" your emotions with your ego mind with stressful analysing. Instead, keep slowly and consciously breathing your human self through your heart where the healing power of your higher consciousness is naturally there to do its work. Trust your natural potential. As human beings, we are designed to feel, and painful emotions soon dissipate so long as they are allowed to flow freely through our own awareness. Being in conflict with what is coming through is what causes difficulty. Letting go and allowing the flow in this way is like giving yourself a big soothing hug. Don't try to make something happen. Instead, open up and allow it to happen.

Let your emotional energy flow through you to be released while at the same time accepting your humanness and the humanness of all others so that you reduce the interference from negative thought-patterns. Don't push this "letting go into healing" process. Let it flow in its own way. This is a form of healing meditation that is subtle, but very effective. You will feel lighter afterwards. You may even have a restful sleep as part of the meditation. This is also effective when you are experiencing a heavy cloud of emotion that does not seem to have any memory or event attached to it. Get back to the exercise when you feel more able.

If it is too challenging for you let go in this way, then it is important to find a therapist who can help you with this process.

2a. *Working with blocks:* If you experience any blocks that prevent you from freely accessing and expressing your thoughts and emotions in your journal, turn your attention to the block and explore that instead. By blocks I mean thoughts or fears that tell you that you shouldn't feel and say those things. For example; you may have been forced to keep silent about family abuse and about your real feelings for fear of being rejected and punished. Write about whatever is blocking you. What does it say? How does it make you feel? Who does it remind you of? Spend some time writing about your relationship with the people involved, and how you were not able to freely express yourself and be heard without fear, judgement, or guilt.

2b. *Getting unstuck:* Reread "Opening the Door to Love" in step 1 on page 9 to remind yourself that you are not wrong just because you have emotions. This will help prepare you to return to part 2 of this exercise, so that you can explore it more fully.

On the other hand, don't think that you have to have some big emotional release. If you feel that there is something there, then stay open to it. It will work its way through in whatever way it is meant to. If you don't feel anything in particular, then that's okay as well. Don't let a lack of emotional release stop you from getting on with the healing process.

3. *Working with the past:* Pay attention to how vulnerable and confused you were at the time of this difficulty, particularly if they are childhood memories. As children, we are naturally powerless and dependent. We have little ability to take real charge of our lives. Feeling abandoned in any way is usually very frightening for us. It is easy to forget how vulnerable and helpless we were as a child. Often, when we look back at our childhood, we do so from an unrealistic adult perspective.

Even in adulthood, we often feel very vulnerable and powerless. We can only work with what we know at the time. It is important that we don't judge ourselves because we didn't know how to deal with situations in the past. Now we have an opportunity to open up the past and learn what we can about it. Learning how to accept ourselves so that we can compassionately care for ourselves is the most important thing. This is how to heal the past and turn it to our advantage.

Allow your emotions to express themselves just as they were back then. If it is a memory of yourself when you were eight-years-old, write as that eight-year-old. This will help you get in touch with how it was for you then.

4. Exploring relationships: Take each person involved in the situation and write down your feelings about each one. For each person, take your time exploring how you felt about them and what these people meant to you. What role did the person in question play in your life? What did you need from this person? If the situation is more recent, does this person remind you of someone from your past? What are the similarities? Remember to let your emotions and thoughts speak freely.

5. Gathering insights: Reflect on the relationship between these past situations and what is going on in your life now.

Have old patterns been repeating themselves? Explore this in your journal.

6. Taking ownership: Open your awareness to how you may have been giving your power away throughout your adulthood by falling into victim thinking. It is very important to be very honest with yourself without judging yourself. Accept full responsibility for your humanness. In other words, let go of any thought that other people should be taking responsibility for your mind/emotional security now as an adult. This is essential for putting yourself in the empowered position of being able to learn and grow through your difficulties; to be able to emotionally stand on your own two feet. Don't be concerned if you don't understand at first how to achieve this. It will come to you as you continue to work with this exercise, read and work through this book, and seek counselling from your mentor. The important thing is being willing to take full ownership of your mind while forgiving yourself for your humanness. Explore changes that you can make in your life that will enable you to break out of any negative patterns that still limit your life. Write down and explore any insights that come to you.

7. Creating your own inner-sanctum: As a part of caring for yourself, use your imagination to spend time exploring how you would have cared for yourself when you were a child or at any other time in your life, as though you are now your own loving, caring and wise parent, guide, and mentor. Today this is in fact the reality. Do this by recalling a significant memory where you felt particularly vulnerable. Focus on this memory and recall it in detail while opening your heart to your vulnerable self in that experience.

When you have a good connection to this memory and the experience of how it was for you then, literally enter this memory as the adult self you are now. Go to your vulnerable human-self/inner-child as this wise and loving guardian and take care of yourself as you know in your heart you needed to be cared for.

You are the one in charge now. This is your mind. This is your memory. Remember to breathe, to let yourself deeply into your heart and explore giving yourself this wonderful gift of love. Do you best to spend quality time just being with your vulnerable self in this way with total acceptance and an open, soft, loving heart. Let your vulnerable self know that he/she belongs to you now and spend time developing this loving connection with yourself. Get to know this vulnerable self within you. Connect to your fears, your dreams and what creates joy in your heart. Let your imagination roam freely in this positive way.

As you come to embrace your inner-child/human-self, feel where your vulnerability is in your body, so that you can be more aware of and tuned in to your human-self. Know that your child-like self is with you always. Know now that you have the power of love to take care of this child-self in any memory that may present itself. Your open heart is your very own inner-sanctum where you facilitate your own healing, growing resilience, and maturity.

7b. Strengthening your connection: As a part of this step, as your vulnerable self, write a letter in your journal to your guardian-self, telling your guardian-self what you need and how you would like to be cared for.

As conscious-awareness, the loving guardian of your vulnerable human-self, write a letter back to your human-self, knowing what your human-self longs to hear from you, the loving guardian.

Let yourself be open to any feelings and insights that may come through, and explore this in your journal as well.

8. Caring For Your Human Self Check List

- Do I provide plenty of space in my life to take care of my vulnerable emotional human-self?
- Do I really have compassion for my human-self?
- Do I impose unrealistic standards or expectations on myself or others that cause me to experience stress and conflict?
- What ways can I reorganise my life so I have the time and space to heal my emotions, clear out my confusion and strengthen my consciousness?
- Am I willing to make this commitment to care for myself an ongoing and essential part of my lifestyle for the sake of my future happiness and wellbeing?
- Can I see that adjusting my lifestyle in this way will help me achieve what I want, rather than be a waste of time?
- Do I have a healthy support network? Am I willing to make the effort to establish one? Am I expecting one person to meet all my needs? Am I taking responsibility to care for my own needs by reaching out to others?
- Am I aware of my needs? Do I truly listen to what my emotions are telling me? Am I willing to take care of my confused inner-child, rather than letting him/her unconsciously run my life, and/or be shut away and neglected?

- What can I do to bring joy, play, recreation into my life?
- Do I appreciate the beautiful, simple things around me like nature and friendship for example?
- Do I take time to appreciate those around me?
- Am I accepting my right to be human and seeing my confusion and mistakes as an opportunity to know myself better and to love myself more?
- Am I aware of what I need in order to ask others to help me meet my needs when this is appropriate? Can I do this without judging their humanness? Am I willing to just have a go and patiently learn about effective communication along the way?
- Am I aware that my humanness is my responsibility to compassionately and lovingly take care of? Am I truly committed to do whatever it takes and learn whatever I need to learn to care for myself and my future?

9. Moving forward: With the help and support of your mentor, spend some time exploring how you can take better care of your vulnerable emotional human self. Use the self-care check list in part 8 to help you in this process. Write about what you need to do in your life now to take better ongoing care of yourself. Do your best to put what you learn through this process into action, while making sure your human self is looked after. Keep using your journal to stay on track with your journey of increasing healing, happiness and fulfilment.

In Summary:
- How do I feel?
- What are my needs?

- How do I try to meet those needs in ways that are healthy or unhealthy?
- In what ways can I take full responsibility to care for myself in conscious, compassionate, and healthy ways.

CHAPTER FOUR SUMMARY

1. Step 3 is learning to process your emotions and undo your confusion on an ongoing basis.
2. Step 3 is the most important step when it comes to changing your life on a deeper level
3. Unfortunately it is the step we most often skip over or do in a half-hearted way. It is the hardest step for the ego to comprehend, because the ego is built on negative conditioning.
4. When we accept the validity of steps 1 and 2, taking personal responsibility to love ourselves unconditionally, and make this approach to life our way of life, a new reality opens up before us.
5. When we are confronted with an emotional challenge, we naturally experience fear, vulnerability and confusion. This initial rush of emotion often overwhelms the ego.
6. Our human-selves are immediately triggered into old habitual ways of coping with these strong emotions in ways that are often self-defeating.
7. Step 3 "Let Go and Tune In", is about building a bridge of healing that enables the human-self to be lifted up into conscious-awareness.
8. Our commitment to face our difficulties, in the spirit of Unconditional Love for our human-selves, opens up a sanctuary within our consciousness for

our trapped emotional energy to safely flow into and through.

9. Indulging in condemnation and blame keeps us trapped in our blind egos and chokes Love out of our hearts.

10. Blame and condemnation prevent us from healing and growing.

11. Blame and condemnation keep us dependent on others to make us happy in a way that never achieves happiness.

12. A fear-based form of power and control that seeks to dominate others has within it the seeds of its own destruction.

13. Ego deludes itself into thinking it has power. True power, that empowers everyone, is found within conscious-awareness.

14. The real power to succeed and be fulfilled rests in the knowing that happiness is a conscious choice, no matter what the situation.

15. Letting go, therefore, is about no longer holding other people, places and things responsible for our happiness.

16. Life skills need to be learned just like anything else, but we won't learn anything else if we are not prepared to let go of, or at least question, our old beliefs.

17. Steps 1 & 2 remind us that there is no-one to blame, not even ourselves. We are just human beings who get confused.

18. Letting go is choosing to NOT focus so much on what is being done to us, but rather to focus on how our minds are reacting to the situation.

19. The fear-based reactions of our survival minds cause our hearts to close. This is a warning sign for our growing conscious-awareness. Instead of shutting down, we must tune into and open up to our human-self/inner-child, while resisting falling into blame and condemnation.

20. Tuning into our feelings and emotions, with the intention to care for ourselves, soon reveals to us the extent to which we have been neglecting ourselves.

21. It is our emotions that tell us when our thinking is constructive or destructive by being either pleasant or painful.

22. While we are condemning ourselves for being human, we become our own worst enemy. We are always going to want to tune out from ourselves and so never get beyond our negative conditioning.

23. Using an effective healing process, we can open our hearts of compassion to our vulnerable human-selves and work constructively with all that flows through our awareness. The strong emotions of our inner-child then flow through us more easily and are healed and released.

24. Attempting to escape from our emotions by trying to "fix" them is driven by fear and will have only limited success.

25. Emotions are meant to be felt and will pass quickly through us if handled in the right way.

26. It is distorted thinking that unnecessarily prolongs painful emotions.

27. Prolonged painful emotions reveal distorted thinking, so by observing the emotions we uncover the distorted thinking.

28. It is the thinking that needs fixing, not the emotions.

29. There are two main tools that can be used to circumvent an inappropriate fight-or-flight reaction, which are also used throughout the day to stay present in our conscious-awareness (mindfulness). They are clarity and slow, full breathing.

30. Following the "feeling trail" often takes us into old memories where the traumas were initially experienced.

31. By opening our compassionate heart to these old painful memories, we add the Unconditional Love that was missing then, which enables healing to occur naturally.

32. Opening our compassionate heart to these old painful memories is like going back in time to take care of our own vulnerable self, who is still stuck in these memories.

33. Our memories now belong to us. As conscious-aware adults we can re-enter our memories and actively care for our vulnerable human-self/inner-child within this mind-space. Our conscious-awareness, therefore, becomes our sanctuary where we can essentially rewrite these memories.

34. We do not truly become adult, where our minds are concerned, until we can consciously take responsibility for our own thoughts and emotions.

35. This process is not about self-pity, it is self-responsibility, self-care.

36. Some of us may find this process difficult at first, having been taught to deny feelings by using anger, for example, to mask our vulnerability.

37. Anger is fear expressed outwardly. We dominate others to feel safe/powerful.

38. Using the right process to clear the emotional backlog from a memory or present situation, creates space for our higher consciousness, in the form of intuitive insight, to enter our awareness.

39. Intuitive insights give us a greater perspective that is more empowering and enables us to deal with issues more skilfully.

40. The mind is very deep and complex. Memories are multi-layered and healing, therefore, can take time and persistence.

41. The garden of the mind will always need looking after. What brings peace and happiness is learning to be a skilled and confident gardener.

42. With confidence we come to realise that the challenges of life are not so much a problem but an opportunity to grow in ever more peace and happiness.

43. Each time we choose to be the representative of Love to our human-selves, we connect even deeper to conscious-awareness.

44. As a result of this deepening connection with our conscious-awareness, in time we feel ourselves being filled with a deep sense of Unconditional Love that seems to come from nowhere.

CHAPTER 5

STEP FOUR
LIVING IN THE NOW

The next stage of the process is putting what we have learnt, and our new choices from that learning, into action every day. This has two important effects. Firstly, by living what we have learnt, we soon discover that there is more to learn. In the process, we gain a better feel for any given issue and can look deeper into it. Secondly, we are able to experience the benefits of our increasing ability to more skilfully take charge of our lives through positive conscious choice. This increasing self-mastery naturally gives us more confidence.

Being aware of the power of consciously and positively working with what every day brings and how essential this is to creating the life that we want, is another vital key to happiness and fulfilment. This next chapter addresses this fundamental law of life.

REALITY IS NOW

NOW is the only time we can act. We can only live our lives in the here and now. Now is where we find the power to create our lives the way we want. Living in the now aligns our life to reality and simplifies it as a result.

As a result of our accumulated confusion, living in the now can be a hard concept to understand and even harder to maintain an ongoing awareness of this reality. Understanding this concept and living it is essential, however, if we want happiness, peace, and fulfilment. So let me explain.

You cannot act yesterday or tomorrow. You may set an important goal for the future, but you can only make your way toward achieving that goal by what you do now, and the now in every day until you get there. What you are experiencing now was created by you with what you thought and did in the past; including the people you have drawn to you. The future, therefore, does not actually exist. It is just a set of possibilities based on what you envision and then put into action on a daily basis. The outcome of your daily action creates your future. This means your future is within your control. If you face, accept, and positively do your best to work with whatever life presents to you in each moment, including your own humanness, a fulfilling future is assured.

Our blind egos also gets confused about the difference between thinking and acting. What we may be thinking now about our future is just that, thinking. It is not our future. It is just our minds thinking. For the same reasons, we cannot change the past. The past is gone. Like the future, the past does not exist except for what resides in our minds' memories. As a result of this confusion regarding thinking and acting, we fall prey to negative mind-states such as worry, regret, guilt, and resentment. I will address this more in the next passage.

When trapped emotional energy is triggered, it may be the result of a trauma from years past, but it is flowing through our consciousness in the now from our memories that are in our minds now. The ego does not understand this.

141

For example, our egos think about something that might happen in the future, or something that may have occurred in the past, or a past memory may be triggered by a situation around us in the now. We then have an emotional reaction to that thought or event and because of this our egos think that something real is occurring. In our confusion, we start to act as if this emotional memory is actually re-occurring around us in our lives now (see "Understanding Emotions on page 69). In reality, we are acting under the influence of a past memory—somewhat like being drunk on that memory! The memory, however, is no more real than watching a movie or reading a novel. It is only occurring within our own minds. A situation around us may be triggering the memory, but it is not causing it. The emotional memory is from the past. Because of this misunderstanding about the nature of the mind, the ego gets lost in its own self-created drama and becomes largely disconnected from the reality of what is really in the now moment. A common result of this confusion is relationship breakdown. We project the ghosts of our past onto the person we are with now.

Our egos do not know how to make use of what the mind has to offer, such as its powerful ability to imagine, for example. As a result, the mind gets lost and out of control. Our imagination can become driven by fear and we can lose touch with what is real. For the average person, much of what the mind is thinking is not about anything that is actually real now. The mind is full of imaginary stories about what we are afraid *might* happen, or what we wish *would* happen, or what we think someone else is thinking, and we are continually acting as though these stories are real. With its confused thinking, the unaware human mind tries to control the uncontrollable and stresses itself out in the process. Effectively and positively harnessing the mind's power is achieved with our conscious–awareness. Our blind egos are not up to the job.

Whether it is emotional healing or achieving your goals, skilfully managing what you are experiencing in the now will determine your future success.

WORRY, REGRET, GUILT, AND RESENTMENT RUINS YOUR FUTURE

One of the things we discover while we are learning to care for our minds is how much time we devote to not accepting the past and worrying about the future. This is a recipe for continual stress. Be certain that worry (or anxiety, a more acute form of worry), regret, guilt, and resentment are a complete waste of time. Not only that, they are the destroyer of a positive future.

I am talking here about prolonged habitual mind–states that trap us into suffering. I am not talking about natural free emotions that prompt us to take responsible care of our lives.

Accepting the Past and Gaining the Benefits

Accepting the past does not mean accepting unacceptable behaviour. The same goes for forgiving others. An essential factor when learning from the past is learning how to honour and care for yourself now.

Forgiveness arises from the awareness that carrying hate and resentment within your mind is self-destructive and keeps you dependent on, and vulnerable to, those you have bad feelings for. You can still say "no" to someone you have forgiven. You can still hold them accountable for their actions if you can, but as I already mentioned, be very aware that seeking justice is not necessarily going to bring healing and a bright future.

Guilt is about *not* forgiving yourself. It comes from not claiming full authority over your own life now. Guilt comes from not acknowledging your human right to make mistakes. Take charge of your life. Learn from your mistakes and move on. That is how to grow and mature. If you have harmed another through your mistakes, then making amends may be important to your moving on, but mentally thrashing yourself is violence and should play no part in this process.

Forgiveness is an important part of the first step of acceptance. Forgiving yourself and others, therefore, is essential for your healing and wellbeing. You are learning to act as an empowered adult, rather than continue to react as an oppressed, helpless and angry child.

Accepting the past and learning from it can transform the way we feel about it. In a way, it does change the past because we are healing our memories. A difficult past, if we can accept it and learn from it, can become a benefit rather than be a burden, because it enables us to grow stronger and wiser.

The Destructive Power of Worry

Worry is taking all the fear and confusion that your human-self has accumulated from the past and creating an imaginary future with it, and a scary one at that. In reality, the ego knows nothing about the possibilities of the future. It only knows its own confused perceptions of the past.

To justify this confused way of thinking, the ego looks into the past and says; "Considering what the past has been for me, I am just being realistic."

The ego even thinks that worrying is being responsible. We think we are doing something tangible by worrying. If we don't worry about a loved one then we think that it means we don't care. Of course it is important to have concern for a loved one, who is in need of help, and to do all we can for them. Worry is different. Worrying is not an action. It is indulging in futile thinking that does not do anything other than harm ourselves. Not only that, worrying does not help our loved ones in the slightest.

Worry disempowers us. It prevents us from clearly seeing what we can positively do now that will take care of our future. It prevents us from letting go once we have done all we can for that moment. Worry never lets us rest and it makes us feel guilty if we do. It makes us a slave to fear and negative conditioning. It is vital to realise the damaging effect worrying has on our minds. As a result of worry, we end up making poor decisions that keep attracting to us the same old unhappy experiences. We become the unhappy authors of our own dramas.

Instead of being lost in our own self-created scary movies, we can look squarely at the reality in front of us and work with it as positively as we can. A large part of the work is sorting out our own human confusion by **paying attention to what we actually can control and what we can't control**. We can sort this through by making two lists under these headings. Examining our worries in our journal is an effective way of bringing the light of reality into the picture. What we can control, we can act on when it is possible to act on it. What we can't control in any given moment, reality dictates that we must let it go. This inner-work is absolutely essential to gaining the clarity to see life in the right perspective.

It would be a safe prediction to say that our future won't be bright if we spend our time worrying and resenting and beating ourselves up with guilt and so on. Our future depends on how we take care of ourselves today and every day.

HUMAN BEINGS LEARN BY TRIAL AND ERROR

Having gained a few insights into the nature of our troubles, our egos have a tendency to think that we has got it all figured out and become attached to this belief. We don't truly know if we have genuinely learned something, however, until we have attempted to put it into action. In doing so, our ego discovers that there is a lot more to learn. Due to false pride, our egos tend to get upset at this and fall into thinking that it is all too hard and that life is unfair. The ego just makes it hard for itself by trying to grasp at the reward without doing the real work.

Unrealistic expectations placed on children to get things right first time is a very sad and common theme. Children often impose these expectations on themselves as well. As a therapist, this is one of the most common stories my clients share with me about their dysfunctional childhood experiences. Once their awareness is awakened to the destructiveness of this unrealistic expectation, it is often a shock to my clients to realise how much their lives have been adversely affected by it.

In reality, one of the most joyful and satisfying experiences a child can have is the freedom and encouragement to explore new things. There is a certain thrill about approaching a new project in various different ways, suffering a bit of frustration at times, but with some gentle guidance and encouragement, finally mastering a new skill. If the parental guidance is appropriate, what the child will remember the most is the excitement of the achievement. All the mistakes and frustrations along the way will not be regarded as a problem. Instead, they will be regarded as the natural stepping–stones to success. As a result of this positive mentoring, the child grows up confident in his/her natural abilities and creative power. Disappointments are taken in one's stride without a sense of reduced self-worth.

How different it is when a child is expected to get a task right the first time. The child is criticised and ridiculed when he/she naturally lacks understanding or stumbles over new challenges of coordination and problem solving. Fear and shame quickly invades the experience. Trying new things soon becomes a source of anxiety. Lack of self-confidence and creativity is the inevitable result, along with a limited ability to effectively face life's challenges.

In reality, trial and error is a natural and essential mode of learning for any human being. Denying this is a fast–track to suffering. Everything takes time to learn, no matter how academically clever we are, and no matter how naturally adept we may be in something.

Playing golf is a good analogy for this. You can digest a library full of golfing books and DVDs, but it is a very different matter when it comes to placing that little white ball onto the tee and slogging it straight and high down the fairway, especially if there is a group of onlookers. If you think learning to play golf is hard, try changing an old ingrained habit, such as regret or worry. It can be done, but it takes time, persistence and a lot of trial and error.

It is impossible to grasp the nuances of such complex tasks in a short time. Repeated experience is required to simply gain awareness of what there is to grasp.

How long did it take you to learn your trade, or to gain your diploma or university degree? How much effort did you put into that? Do you think mastering your human mind is going to be any easier? Think again. It is your life's work, and be sure that everything else in your life depends on it. Being skilful at caring for your mind in the now is the foundation of all your happiness and wellbeing in every area of your life.

Be very aware, therefore, of when you are being hard on yourself for not getting things "right". Fully mastering some deep issues may not even be possible in your lifetime, but learning to skilfully manage these issues certainly is possible. Other issues go less deep, and with persistence, can be completely overcome.

I am routinely helping people to manage and to even overcome self-defeating behaviours, just as I have overcome the chronic depression of my past. Often more orthodox therapists have given up on these people. My clients are often told that medication is their only solution. I have had the pleasure of showing them otherwise.

To achieve this success, each of these people has learned to accept and care for their human-self, using their own adapted variations of this powerful process. Their success was assured because they did not give up. They have learned to open their awareness to what is in front of them in each moment and make the most of it.

DISCIPLINE, ONE DAY AT A TIME.

Putting this process into action requires discipline. Discipline in the form of persistence, determination and structure is essential for facing life's challenges and creating the life you want. Discipline brings with it freedom to be who you want to be, but only if this discipline is in the spirit of self-acceptance.

Discipline is about setting goals, making plans, creating routines and then sticking by them. It is about your commitment to your life. This brings forth the power of your potential and an opportunity to gain more awareness of how to care for your vulnerable human-self.

Unfortunately, for many people, the word discipline brings up bad memories of being dominated by unskilful parents or other authority figures. When a child is disciplined with unrealistic expectations and harsh judgment, necessary guidance becomes oppressive and soul-destroying. The child either gives up or rebels or becomes an unthinking conformist or a stressed out perfectionist. Depression, anger and anxiety are common consequences.

When the discipline is erratic and contradictory, the child becomes confused, scattered, angry and fearful. There can be a lack of consistency in adult life, leading to many disappointments. The individual's character can often lack sincerity, trust and trustworthiness, due to not having someone to rely on as a child.

When the child gets too little discipline and is left alone too often without positive mentoring, there develops a shallowness and a lack of commitment. Depression and various habits of trying to escape life may develop because the child didn't learn how to push through with difficult tasks.

When discipline is rightly employed, our conscious-awareness develops a great strength of will that serves our highest good. Setting up and persisting with daily routines such as reading, journaling and meditating, as a process of caring for our human-selves, for example, develops an ability to stay above our old negative conditioning. With persistence, new life-sustaining habits are built into our minds, over-writing our old self-defeating habits. As I mentioned in the previous chapter, it can be hard work at first, but it gets increasingly easier as time goes by, because, with persistence, our level of skill naturally increases and the new good habits take over.

Discipline is also much easier when you divide it into small chunks. Life is lived in small moments, which go together to make a bigger moment like a day or a week. Conserve your energy by focusing on NOW. Do the best you can in the moment you have. Every small effort is taking you forward. Mistakes are no problem. When accepted and used as learning opportunities, they help guide you forward. Only giving up or beating yourself up is taking you nowhere. Tomorrow is a new day. There is always a new opportunity to put into practice what you have learned from the previous moment.

Focusing on and making the most of this moment sets you up in the best possible way for the next moment. Even if you make a complete mess of one moment, you always have the next moment to try again, armed with what you have learned. There is no tomorrow to worry about. There is only now. When tomorrow comes, it will be a new set of now moments to apply your ongoing process to. If you want to climb a mountain, start with the rock in front of you, and then the next one and so on. If you continue to look up at the peak and allow yourself to keep being daunted by it, you are likely to give up. It is how we do the journey, including taking care of our human-selves along the way, that makes all the difference. Reaching the peak is then an inevitable reality.

Goal Setting

When we set a goal, we are focusing ourselves on a definite course of action. In the course of trying to create this particular outcome, we inevitably run into obstacles in the form of other people, physical and environmental limitations and, in particular, our own negative conditioning. This unpredictability must be accepted as part of the journey.

To our unaware egos, this can be a source of frustration and inevitable conflict. The ego thinks events should unfold precisely the way that it wants. Our egos, however, are just being grandiose. Our egos often think we have some sort of godly powers over life, the universe and everything. But then in the next moment, we think we have no power at all, because we start blaming others when things go wrong. We don't like accepting that we are human and therefore often confused and unaware, just like the other human beings we are relying on to help us achieve our goals. This is reality. It is an inevitable and natural part of the journey.

We cannot know all the variables. The outcome of any goal is in many ways unpredictable. Rather than getting attached to the outcome that we think is necessary, we need to be open to positively working with whatever the moment brings. This positive approach brings inevitable success, but not always in the form we expect.

The more we accept what comes to us in every moment, including our humanness, and positively work with it, the more efficient our journey to our goal will be. While we are working toward accomplishing a chosen goal, we are learning, healing and growing along the way.

Setting goals is essential for giving your life conscious direction. Goals can be short, medium or long term. If we don't take responsibility for our direction in life, we risk being taken over by our negative conditioning and also by other people's agendas. We risk not paying attention to what feels right for ourselves.

Regularly keeping track of your goals and your progress in your journal is essential to success. If you don't, it is very easy to get distracted and forget your intentions. Six months later, you may suddenly remember the goal that you set for yourself and wonder how you lost track of it.

Using your journal in this way is like managing a business, your life business. A manager is lost without his/her work dairy and frequent staff meetings that keep track of progress and problems. Your mind is like your staff, who you have been given the responsibility to manage.

Creating Routines

Routines are essential for ensuring that your journey toward your goal stays on track. For instance, getting up earlier than normal may help you achieve your goals (I wouldn't get my writing done without doing just that!). Your human body/mind may not agree with this routine, but your conscious-awareness, utilizing your will, must override this. To carry this extra load you may also need to improve your diet and get to bed earlier. You create this new routine and keep it consistent by using your conscious-awareness.

The old habits will naturally resist. The primal body/mind is a habit-bound creature. Habit forming is important for survival and efficiency. It gives our conscious-awareness less to think about so it can get on with more important things. When it comes to changing a habit, it is you as conscious-awareness who must make this happen. The new habit must be burnt into the brain's synaptic pathways while the old habits are erased. In order to erase these old habits, we must go against them. It means driving through them with the new program. To use the previous example, getting out of bed earlier than usual might feel like pushing against a heavy object. We may literally need to let out a roar of galvanized strength and determination to push our human-selves out of bed. In order to achieve our goals, that are envisaged and created by our conscious-awareness so that we can express and achieve our potential, we must not let ourselves be controlled by our old, blind, habit-bound minds that cling to the same old ways.

Your body/mind is your vehicle in this life. You, as conscious-awareness, are the driver. It is like riding a horse. You train your horse and guide your horse, not the other way around. A well-trained horse knows what to do in a way that is in harmony with the rider, but the rider must ultimately be in control. In order to achieve your goals, you must take full responsibility for what is required. You must implement self-empowering behaviours and persist with them until they become the new habits. Routines are essential, therefore, for creating new life-enhancing habits. After all, that is how your conditioning was created in the first place.

Of course, in the process of galvanizing our will and pushing through with the new routine, it is important not to push ourselves too hard. There must be a balance between nurturing ourselves and expanding ourselves. When we extend ourselves, we often trigger old emotional wounds that can start to undermine our progress. This is one of the challenges of discipline. This must be accepted. Time out needs to be taken to process and heal these old wounds in order to gain the strength to push forward once again. Slow and steady wins the race when dealing with our humanness, otherwise we are likely to give up, or if we keep driving through regardless, we could burn out.

Reading, journaling and meditating, for example, needs to be set to a routine as much as possible to ensure that time is created for it.

Of course routines, as well as goals and plans, may need to be adjusted occasionally as we gain more awareness of what is best for us along the way.

JOY AND SERENITY IS NOW

Despite what our egos think, true joy and serenity is not found by getting what we want in the material world. This may satisfy us for a while, but then the mind soon takes its gains for granted and starts looking for something else. This also includes relationships. True joy and serenity, and even fulfilment, is found by transcending the mind's propensity for holding other people, places and things responsible for our happiness. This treasure of treasures is found in the stillness of being present in the now while accepting everything as it is. The stillness and its accompanying peace arises to the degree that we stop fighting reality as it is. Even as our human minds continue to react, we can consciously stop, rest in our open, flowing breath and observe, while allowing all this reaction to flow through us, knowing that this disturbance is not our true Self. We can even get to the point of having a bit of a laugh at our silly human-selves as we gets ourselves all tangled up yet again, like a parent lovingly laughing at the antics of a beloved child.

We suffer because we think that we can't bear this or we can't live without that. When we consciously step back and look within ourselves in the spirit of self-acceptance and Personal Responsibility, when we can stay still and observe the anxiety that is flowing through us without being so pulled into it, we have a chance of seeing that the anxiety has no real foundation.

Without the guiding principles of Unconditional Love and Personal Responsibility, consciousness has no real power and descends into being mere ego. Without the power of this greater knowing, the ego is held captive and under the control of the confusion and primal instincts of the human-self. The human-self, without the guiding power of an awakened consciousness, only displays the pseudo power of fight-or-flight. This lower level of being is reflected in all the misguided behaviour that causes suffering in this world.

When we empower our detached and observing conscious-awareness by seeing ourselves as the loving guardian of our vulnerable humanness, a new level of inner-strength is available to us. A key aspect of the power of conscious-awareness comes from the fact that it operates in the present moment, above and beyond all past conditioning and human limitations. It is infinitely adaptable. This power that is our consciousness is always available to us. Within this aware consciousness is the knowing that no matter what comes and goes in the turbulent human mind, consciousness can remain still and tranquil, ready to act. From consciousness comes our ability to observe our life from a higher perspective

If this greater self was not a true reality then of course we would just be deluding ourselves. Any attempt to live this process, no matter how dedicated we may be, would have little or no benefit. This is not the case, however.

When we accept ourselves as we are and do our best to be the loving guardian for our humanness on a daily basis, we are actively creating a sanctuary of loving kindness, forgiveness, acceptance, clarity, commitment and so on for our vulnerable human minds to flow into and through. In effect, we have created a controlled environment within our conscious-awareness that insulates us from the negativity of the world around us, and even the negativity of our own conditioning.

Joy is a natural result of being centred in conscious-awareness. Joy, flowing from the heart of consciousness, does not depend on the conditions and circumstances of our everyday changing human affairs. When centred in conscious-awareness, even when we are in the midst of a difficult challenge, joy can be found.

This aware detachment from the mind does not cut us off from the world—the opposite in fact. We are in the world, interacting with it, but less likely to be thrown off centre by it. As a result, we see the reality of things more clearly and can respond to the world around us more effectively. We have taken command of our own minds. We are now creating our own reality, a reality that is in tune with the higher laws of consciousness, regardless of how out of tune everyone else is. Study the lives of people like Mahatma Gandhi or Nelsen Mandela and you will have a graphic example of what I mean.

Mahatma Gandhi (2-10-1869 – 30-1-1948) provided us with a great example of this power of conscious-awareness. His faith in unconditional love and total personal responsibility was unwavering. This one skinny little man was able to unshackle India from its unjust subjugation by the British Empire without the use of brute force. He also managed to calmly and constructively direct the volatile passions of the Indian masses.

His greatest weapon was his own self-awareness process. His final act of passive resistance that broke the back of Britain's control over India was achieved through weeks of meditation. While Indian statesmen were waiting impatiently for their leader, Gandhi, to offer them insights as to what to do next, Gandhi simply continued to meditate and contemplate. Finally he came up with a strategy that was so simple and yet so powerful that only a supreme consciousness could have known of the potential of the act. I encourage you to study the life of Mahatma Gandhi. You will learn much from his example. A quick way to do this is to watch the Academy Award winning movie ("Gandhi") that was made about his life. I recommend this to all my students.

Our conscious-awareness has a greater power to love. This is the power to love unconditionally. This is the ultimate power. This true love is difficult for the ego to grasp. Ego is created out of conditioned love. Unconditional love can even scare the ego because true love can see straight through the ego's facade. In contrast, the hearts of those who are humble and wise (which is a deep, quiet inner-strength born out of self-acceptance) know this greater love as their foundation in life.

Joy and serenity is within your power to create here and now, regardless of your circumstances in life. It is the very core of your being, your true home and refuge from the confusion of this world and your own human mind.

Our emotions and feelings are telling our conscious-awareness vital information that we need to know in each moment. They are there to prompt our conscious-awareness to pause, to observe, and to assess the reality of the situation, rather than blindly react from old fearful imaginings, like our egos do.

As we put steps 1, 2, and 3, into practice, we can *feel* what is going on within us and know, or at least discover, what these feelings mean in relation to caring for our vulnerable humanness and honouring our potential.

When we accept that our life is a journey of continual learning, growing and awakening, we can then harmoniously work with what comes our way. We are no longer in such conflict with the circumstances and conditions of our lives, or so emotionally dependent on things happening the way our egos think they should. We can see that every moment is an opportunity to accept our humanness, to know ourselves better, and to gain a greater mastery of ourselves. We can be more aware of what our human minds are doing with that moment and how we get ourselves all tangled up and lost. We can relax into the moment we are in and see the benefits that are there for us. We can step forward with our conscious-awareness, our open heart, and be the skilful manager of our lives in every now moment.

EXERCISE 5:
EMBRACING THE DAY

Ongoing Self Maintenance

Establishing and maintaining the right attitude toward each new day, regardless of what challenges may lay ahead, is essential for continued growth, for increasing inner-harmony and for successfully achieving your goals.

What this means is that you will be using the skills that you have learned so far in this book in a summarised daily process. At times though, the challenges that you face in your life may be such that they take up much of your attention, and much of your process work will be focused on these issues. You may be in the process of trying to survive each day as you battle through these major challenges.

There is a tendency, however, to drop our personal growth work when the crisis is over, which leaves us unprepared for the next major challenge. As a result, we tend to lurch from one crisis to the next. This roller-coaster ride can be reduced, or even avoided, by maintaining a daily self-awareness process, such as I am going to lay out here.

This process of embracing each day is usually done in the evening or first thing in the morning. This will of course require discipline. For example, if processing in the morning, getting to bed earlier and setting the alarm to get up earlier may be required. Such discipline may be tough at first, but the energy-saving benefits of consistently sticking to this process will soon compensate.

Of course not everyone's circumstances and schedules will allow for doing this work first thing in the morning. Doing the work at some other time in the day or evening will still work, providing it is consistent.

This constructive approach to your daily affairs covers four main areas, which are: ***Acceptance and Responsibility, Gratitude/Connection, Clarity*** and ***Ongoing Awareness.***

Acceptance and Responsibility

1) If you are in conflict with what is going on in your life, in other words, if you see yourself as a victim, you are not in the optimal position to successfully work through whatever challenges you may have or may think you have. I say "may think you have" as a reminder that most issues are really created imaginings, that we project onto life, that are not real at all. When you believe you are a victim, you are actually denying your potential as an empowered being of conscious–awareness. You cut yourself

off from the power and knowing of your higher-consciousness.

2) Know that everything that comes your way today is an opportunity for you to grow. See all things as ultimately beneficial to you and not as a problem, or as unfair. To work with life and overcome your challenges, you must accept it as it is. You must be willing to step up and face it squarely. Take some deep breaths, therefore, and prepare yourself to let in, without resistance, all that faces you this day, including your own human vulnerabilities, with compassion and with courage.

Gratitude/Connection

3) Before the practical part of this exercise begins, spend some time raising your awareness of what you have to be grateful for. An "attitude of gratitude" is an essential step up to connecting to your higher-consciousness. Looking for the good in your life lifts your consciousness to a more constructive and motivated frame of mind. It will also remind you that just a shift in focus can make all the difference when it comes to having a positive frame of mind.

4) Open up your journal and make a list of what you have to be grateful for and spend some minutes contemplating on this. Don't just look for big or special things. Have a more aware look at the everyday mundane things that you may take for granted.

5) Other ways of lifting your consciousness are achieved by reading some inspirational literature, meditation and music, or whatever helps you to connect to your own inner-sanctum.

6) This will help to empower your consciousness so that you can see/feel the reality of things more clearly.

Clarity

7) To begin the practical part of this process, make a spontaneous list of what is ahead of you this day.

8) When this is done, examine each point and separate *fact* from *fiction*. The facts are the things that you actually know, such as a bill you need to pay or a job interview you need to attend. Fiction is all the worry that your ego's imagination may add to the mix, such as convincing yourself that the person who is to interview you for the job is bound to reject you. For more information see Exercise 3 on page 86.

9) Create two separate lists—one for the facts, and one for the fiction. Separating the content of what you have previously written in this way will help you to process it.

10) Re-examine your fact and fiction lists and expand and refine them if you need to.

11) Using the "fiction" list, under the Heading of "Vulnerabilities", spend some time writing about any fear or concern that you may have about what lies ahead of you this day.

12) Knowing that you are conscious-awareness, the representative of Unconditional Love to your human-self, spend some time processing these thoughts and emotions with an open compassionate heart. This will help you to redirect this vulnerability through your conscious-awareness throughout the day, while at the same time being able to stay above it enough to act consciously and constructively. Refer to Exercise 4 on page 123.

13) Don't forget to keep your breath open and flowing as an essential part of the process of channelling and welcoming your human-self into your heart of consciousness.

14) Now revisit your fact list and get in touch with how you are going to plan out your day. Draw yourself up a quick schedule and a list of things you need to remember. Bear in mind that this will just be a working plan, which will no doubt need altering as the day unfolds.

15) Often, what you thought would be a straightforward task ends up taking far longer than expected. Sometimes something unforeseen occurs that demands a greater priority over what you had previously planned. It is essential, therefore, to be flexible.

16) This plan, nonetheless, will give you some good direction and allow you to be much more aware than you would normally be.

Ongoing awareness

17) Throughout the day, frequently refer to what you have written in regards to your schedule and other reminders, as well as any fear and insecurity that you were able to identify from within your vulnerable humanness.

18) Throughout the day, use your open, conscious breath as a way to stay in tune with your whole self. Stop, breath and let yourself into your awareness. Pay attention to what you are feeling so that you can stay in touch with your human-self with your conscious-awareness.

19) Now you have raised your conscious-awareness to what your day may have in store. You have also prepared yourself to be in tune with the needs of your vulnerable human-self. You will be in a better position to deal with the unexpected, and also your own negative conditioning that can threaten your balance.

20) As conscious-awareness, you have the power to take charge of your day, to embrace it as a most precious gift from life.

CHAPTER FIVE SUMMARY

1. We don't truly know if we have genuinely learned something until we have attempted to put it into action.

2. The ego's pride tends to get upset and falls into self-rejection, blame, or denial when things don't live up to our expectations. This makes our path of personal growth unnecessarily hard.

3. When we accept that our life is a journey of continual learning, growth and awakening, we can then work harmoniously with what comes our way, rather than be in conflict with it.

4. You can only manage your life in the now. You cannot act yesterday or tomorrow.

5. Whether it is emotional healing, or achieving your goals, skilfully managing what you are experiencing in every moment will determine your success.

6. Worry, regret, guilt and resentment are a complete waste of time. Not only that, they are the destroyer of a positive future.

7. An essential factor in learning from the past is learning how to honour yourself and care for yourself now.

8. Accepting the past does not mean accepting unacceptable behaviour.

9. We can still say no to someone we have forgiven.

10. You can still hold people accountable for their actions if you can, but be very aware that seeking justice is not necessarily going to bring you healing and a bright future.

11. Carrying hate and resentment within your mind is self–destructive and keeps you dependent on and vulnerable to those you have resentment towards.

12. Guilt is about not forgiving yourself. Acceptance is another word for forgiveness.

13. A difficult past can become a benefit rather than be a burden because, when faced, it can enable us to grow become stronger and more mature.

14. Worry is taking all the fear and confusion that your human-self has accumulated from the past and creating an imaginary future with it.

15. In reality, the ego knows nothing about the possibilities of the future. The ego is the unhappy author of its own drama.

16. The inner-work of sorting out our own human confusion, by paying attention to and taking compassionate responsibility for what we are feeling, enables us to have the clarity to see the reality of what is in front of us.

17. Our future depends on how we take care of today, everyday.

18. Unrealistic expectations placed on children to get things right first time can have a deep negative impact on the rest of their lives.

19. Suffering under the pressure of such unrealistic expectations means fear and shame quickly invades the experience of learning, and trying new things soon becomes a source of anxiety.

20. In reality, one of the most joyful and satisfying experiences a child can have is the freedom and encouragement to explore new things.

21. If the parental guidance is appropriate, what the child will remember the most is the excitement of the achievement. The child grows up confident in his/her natural abilities and creative power. Disappointments

are taken in one's stride without a sense of reduced self-worth.

22. Everything takes time to learn, no matter how academically clever we are and no matter how naturally adept we may be at something.

23. Being skilful at caring for your mind is the foundation for all your happiness and wellbeing.

24. Discipline in the form of persistence, determination and structure is essential for facing life's challenges and creating the life that you want.

25. Discipline brings with it freedom to be who you want to be, but only if this discipline serves the heart, the greater principles of your higher-consciousness.

26. Unfortunately, for many people, the word discipline brings up bad memories of being dominated by unskilful parents or other authority figures.

27. When discipline is rightly employed, our conscious-awareness develops a great strength of will that serves our highest good.

28. Setting up and persisting with daily routines such as reading, journaling and meditating, as a process of caring for our human-self, develops an ability to stay above the old confusions and creates new life-sustaining habits.

29. Turning our life around can be hard at first, but as our life-sustaining habits become stronger and begin to overtake our old negative habits, life gets increasingly easier.

30. Discipline is much easier when you divide your time up into small chunks. Life is lived in small moments, which go together to make a bigger moment like a day or a week.

31. Conserve your energy by focusing on NOW. Every small effort is taking you forward. Only giving up or beating yourself up is taking you nowhere.

32. Aware consciousness is the knowing that no matter what comes and goes in the turbulent mind, consciousness can remain still and tranquil, ready to act.

33. Joy flows naturally from the heart of conscious-awareness, even in the midst of a difficult challenge.

34. Consciousness is like a higher will. In order for it to be a powerful force in our lives, it must be activated. We must actively exercise our power of choice and parent our human-selves.

35. If we don't face our fears, we don't access the power that enables us to transform our lives.

36. Those who are humble (which is a deep, quiet inner-strength) and wise know Unconditional Love as their foundation in life.

CHAPTER 6

STEP FIVE
LIVE THE PROCESS
AS A WAY OF LIFE

Human beings have a tragic habit of refusing to take responsibility for the content of their own minds. We are like a car being driven by a confused teenager who does not have the skills to drive that car and who refuses to accept the reality of the road rules. When we keep crashing into things, we blame everybody else for the problem. When we are not blaming others for our poor driving skills, we are judging ourselves as unworthy, but do nothing or very little to learn better driving skills. However, this does not fit with the rules of the road, the rules of life. Adult human beings are meant to emotionally stand on their own two feet. Instead we judge and blame to avoid facing the pain and confusion that has accumulated in our minds, and punish ourselves and others when we can't avoid this pain. The result, of course, is just more pain. Worse still, we keep passing this pain and confusion down the line from generation to generation. Continuing on in this way ensures that we stay blind to reality and thus never discover the natural laws of life that create peace, harmony, love, and fulfilment in our lives.

Actively taking loving care of our own humanness is a fundamental way to effectively awaken our consciousness to this higher reality, simply because love is the only thing that heals. By consciously caring for our own minds, we get a direct experience of what works in all relationship dynamics.

It is not about having to get it right all the time. It is about accepting the validity of these ideals and being willing to have a go at *being* these ideals as best we can every day for the rest of our lives. Any step further along this path brings benefit to our lives. If we persist, despite the confusions of our human-selves, we soon discover how incredibly beautiful life can be, even with the occasional pain and struggle. Getting it right is a matter of a naturally-growing self-mastery, born out of trial and error and a commitment to never give up on ourselves.

It is our stuck child-selves that say we should be magically happy without actually making the effort to learn how to create happiness in our lives. In our confusion, we can still be unconsciously waiting for mum and dad to finish the job, but this is not going to happen, and there is grieving we all have to go through around this. Our current loved ones can't do the job for us either. It is too much for one human being to take on that job for another.

Because of our lack of faith and trust in ourselves, we also have trouble trusting others. We only tend to give self-improvement programs half an effort at the most, and then say, "See, I told you it wasn't going to work." Step 5 urges us to confront this confused thinking and finally see that it is this type of thinking that robs us of the life that we deep down know we can have.

We are freer to get serious and take responsibility for our lives when we accept that it is okay to be human. Accepting our humanness also means accepting that we have naturally got what it takes to overcome our problems, even though we don't at first know how to access our natural potential. If we never give up, and refuse to see failure as defeat, but instead just another opportunity to grow, we will find the personal power to manage anything that life can throw at us. In fact, feeling such personal power becomes exciting, and personal growth becomes a natural way of life.

Freedom is a state of mind. You can be restricted physically beyond your control, but your human mind is totally your own. The way you take care of your mind has enormous influence on every aspect of your life. The relationship between your consciousness and the rest of your being, higher and lower, is your life's foundation. From this perspective, life is definitely what you make it. Therefore, from this moment on, take your mind into your own hands as best you can and step into the positive flow of life and start living. If you persist no matter what, you will be amazed by the results.

Step 5 is about recognizing and accepting that life is a journey of continual growth in wisdom and maturity. When we accept this level of responsibility for our lives, the key to creating the life that we want is in our hands.

APPENDIX ONE

EMOTION	DEFINITION
Fear	Feeling in danger of something that may be real or imagined.
Anger	Aggressively reacting over loss of control of someone or something.
Anxiety	Fear of not knowing what is going to happen next.
Panic	Acute anxiety.
Hurt	Feeling that someone has deliberately wronged me.
Confusion	Not understanding what is going on.
Frustration	Reacting over loss of control of someone or something.
Depression	Feeling trapped, powerless, unworthy—internally and externally.
Self-pity	Feeling victimised by life.
Loneliness	Feeling empty and isolated.
Guilt	Feeling responsible for another's pain or imagined pain.
Grief	Unwilling to accept losing something I am attached to.

Worry	Dwelling on imaginary negative scenarios that cause fear.
Resentment	Need to punish others for perceived wrongs.
Hate	Need to deliberately harm others for perceived wrongs.
Embarrassment	Feeling like a fool.
Shame	Feeling that I am fundamentally no good as a person.
Sadness	Feeling loss of fulfillment and disconnected from the joys of life.
Numbness	Unable to feel due to being overwhelmed. Sensory overload.
Shock	Acute sensory and emotional overload.
Boredom	Lacking inspiration.
Apathy	An uncaring disconnection from a situation.
Rejection	Feeling unsupported by those important to me.
Abandonment	Feeling deserted by those important to me.
Longing	Feeling separated from an important source of fulfillment.
Jealousy	Wanting what someone else has.
Betrayed	Feeling that someone important to me has deliberately broken my trust in them.
Self-condemnation	Concluding that I don't measure up, that I am unworthy of love.
Regret	Wishing something that did happen, didn't happen.
Self-righteousness	Feeling that I am right and others are wrong and in need of correcting by me— thinking I am superior—playing God.

Shyness	Feeling that I am not good enough to stand out.
Stubbornness	Unwilling to see beyond my narrow point of view.
Rebelliousness	Wanting to react against someone I perceive as doing wrong.
Over —rationalisation	Perceiving from a narrow intellectual perspective that is disconnected from higher intuition.

APPENDIX TWO

EMOTION	MOVING FROM VICTIM TO EMPOWERMENT
Fear	I have faith in life's higher purpose—my Higher-Self.
Anger	I take responsibility for my own happiness.
Anxiety	I accept that every moment is an opportunity to grow.
Panic	I breath deeply and slowly and stay aware in the moment and trust that I can work with my circumstances one day at a time.
Hurt	I accept Total Personal Responsibility to Love myself Unconditionally.
Confusion	I honour my own needs by compassionately caring for my human-self.
Frustration	I solve my problems by practicing cooperation and negotiation with clear, open, and patient communication.
Depression	I take loving care of myself by acting on the truth that I am totally worthy.
Self-pity	I accept compassionate responsibility for my emotions.

Loneliness	I accept Total Personal Responsibility to Love myself Unconditionally with the knowing that Love attracts Love.
Guilt	I follow my own heart, knowing that it is for the highest good of all, even when others don't agree.
Grief	I take responsibility for my future happiness, and trust life's higher purpose.
Worry	I create a positive future by taking responsibility for my life now and give to my Higher-Self what I have no control over now.
Resentment	I am responsible for my own happiness.
Hate	I take responsibility for my own emotional pain and accept that everyone is an essential part of Light/Life/Love like me.
Embarrassment	I accept my right to be human and Love myself as I am.
Shame	I accept my right to be human and Love myself as I am.
Sad	I accept and stay open to my emotions and share them with others, while at the same time accept responsibility to care for them myself.
Numb	I am learning to breathe, be open and allow all that I feel to freely flow through me. As conscious-awareness I have great potential.
Shock	I stay open and flexible to sudden changes in life, knowing that by caring for myself I am capable of working through anything.
Boredom	I accept full responsibility to create my life according to my heart's highest choice and I am willing to learn what it takes to do this.

Apathetic	I find opportunities to give selfless service knowing that I am a gift of Life being offered to this world.
Rejection	I accept loving responsibility for my own self-worth and happiness.
Abandoned	I look within for the source of my personal security. I accept Total Personal Responsibility to Love myself Unconditionally.
Longing	I accept my present circumstances as ultimately perfect for my personal growth.
Jealous	I take responsibility for my own fears and insecurities.
Betrayed	I stay humble enough to see that other people have needs and fears just like I do, and I take responsibility for my own needs.
Self-condemnation	I accept that my mistakes are simply opportunities to grow, and therefore a natural part of my journey. My worthiness is absolute.
Regret	I accept past difficulties as opportunities to grow and therefore learn from the lessons of my past for the sake of my future.
Self-righteousness	I take responsibility for my own emotional pain and accept that everyone is an essential and equal part of Light/Life/Love like me.
Shyness	I take responsibility for my own potential to shine.
Stubborn	I face my fears so I can step outside my comfort zones and into freedom, into a world and universe beyond my limited imagination.
Rebellious	I realise that I am a reflection of the very thing I am rebelling against. Instead I learn the power of cooperation and forgiveness.

Over—rationalisation	I choose not to look for quick answers, knowing Life is far greater than I can imagine. I open my mind, observe and feel and let Life be my teacher. Intuitive feeling is the doorway to higher perception.

ABOUT THE AUTHOR

Phil began his own journey of personal and spiritual development in 1984, motivated by his need to overcome chronic depression. Having succeeded in his goal of overcoming depression, Phil continued to explore the path of self-awareness and self-empowerment, awakening and developing his natural abilities in this area. It was then a natural progression to find himself helping others with their healing and personal development with one to one counselling and group work.

Over the years, Phil privately studied Existential Psychology, Theosophy, Buddhism, Metaphysics, and Hands-on Healing. He also completed a degree on the subject of Human Consciousness at the University of Queensland, which included Jungian and General Psychology. Phil now works as a psychotherapist at his own counselling and complimentary therapies center in Brisbane. He teaches and writes on the subject of personal and spiritual development using, amongst other frameworks, the 5 Step Process, which he developed himself. The 5 Step Process is closely aligned to the school of Psychosynthesis, developed by Dr Robert Assigioli. Phil is also teaches self-awareness and meditation using contemporary Buddhist and Theosophical frameworks as well as the 5 Step Process.

He is a dedicated practitioner of his own spiritual and personal healing, integration and development, which he regards as his most important source of training as a therapist and personal development teacher. He regards his life as a living meditation, seeking harmony with life on every level, allowing all life's experiences to be his teacher. Phil lives in Brisbane, Australia, with his wife and two step daughters.

Contact Information
For inquiries about counseling, coaching, groups, workshops, courses, seminars contact:

Inner Harmony Center
142 Apollo Rd. Bulimba 4171
Queensland, Australia.
Ph: (07) 33997876
E-mail: info@innerharmony.com.au
Internet: http://www.innerharmony.com.au